Jesus
of
Arabia

ANDREW THOMPSON

Illustrations by Teresa Penman

Jesus of Arabia

Christ through
Middle Eastern Eyes

ROWMAN & LITTLEFIELD
Lanham • Boulder • New York • London

Published by Rowman & Littlefield
A wholly owned subsidiary of The Rowman & Littlefield Publishing Group, Inc.
4501 Forbes Boulevard, Suite 200, Lanham, Maryland 20706
www.rowman.com

Unit A, Whitacre Mews, 26-34 Stannary Street, London SE11 4AB, United Kingdom

British Library Cataloguing in Publication Information Available

Library of Congress Cataloging-in-Publication Data Available
ISBN 978-1-5381-0944-1 (cloth : alk. paper)
ISBN 978-1-5381-0945-8 (electronic)

♾️™ The paper used in this publication meets the minimum requirements of American National Standard for Information Sciences—Permanence of Paper for Printed Library Materials, ANSI/NISO Z39.48-1992.

Printed in the United States of America

I dedicate this book to my wife Navina.

She has opened my eyes to the treasures of the Scriptures through her cultural sensitivity. Because of her insights, my understanding of Eastern and Western interpretations has deepened; as a result I am enriched beyond measure.

CONTENTS

PART FOUR: LANGUAGE

PART FIVE: THE ELEPHANT IN THE ROOM

FOREWORD

T HE MOST CURSORY INSPECTION of the tenets of different faiths reveals considerable common ground among them. In all faiths a respect for human life, a desire for peace and safety, and an imperative to appreciate each other as valued individuals, guides adherents in living worthy lives. An understanding that our life on earth is not our ultimate existence unites faiths. Therefore we must be thoughtful and upright in the way we live in order to realize the potential for broad human development around the globe.

Uniting people of differing faiths, finding common ground among those who come from different cultural traditions, harnessing the core values that are common to all religions – these principles are consistent with the aims of the United Arab Emirates. Following the vision of our Founding President, the late Sheikh Zayed bin Sultan Al Nahyan, and continuing under the wise leadership of His Highness the President of the UAE and Ruler of Abu Dhabi, Sheikh Khalifa bin Zayed al Nahyan, the UAE has committed itself to bridging the gaps that separate people of different cultures, and discovering and celebrating the bonds that unite them. We believe strongly that honest, good faith dialogue among dedicated individuals and organizations representing people of diverse religions, cultures, beliefs and backgrounds can help make this a better, more peaceful and more prosperous world.

In this new book Andrew Thompson confronts two facts, Islam and Christianity, and responds with imagination, ingenuity, candour, and courage. Though deeply committed to Christianity, Thompson is in no way proselytizing for his faith. His global and all-inclusive vision enables him to breach barriers that normally block rational consideration of Islam and Christianity together. He reveals his vision explicitly when he comments on the words of Jesus: 'My Kingdom is not of this world.' Thompson writes that 'the Kingdom of God is a people who transcend nationality, nations, races, religion, and even time itself.'

This generous vision should assure readers that Thompson is welcoming them all to his majlis. Much like the way that the Emperor Akbar sought to understand and appreciate many different religious views by inviting their spokesmen to his sixteenth-century Mughal court, Thompson reads sacred texts with close regard to the prevailing ideas and assumptions of their settings and so creates an enlightening conversation about their meaning. His hospitality brings Muslims and Christians alike to seats of honour.

By placing Biblical texts, especially the Gospels, in an Arab context, Thompson juxtaposes scriptural and anthropological evidence in a startlingly informative fashion. His bold use of Mark Allen's *jizz* categories provides a comfortable way for organizing vast and varied flocks of evidence. Thompson's sympathetic and personally informed commentary will be particularly appreciated by readers unfamiliar with Arab culture.

The Qur'an and the life of the Prophet Muhammad (Peace Be Upon Him) figure prominently in Thompson's effort to enlarge and refine an understanding of Jesus (Peace Be Upon Him). Thompson's respect for Islam allows him to present a vision that does indeed embrace Muslims and give them new insights into their own culture and beliefs.

I join the Reverend Canon Thompson in his hope that this book will stimulate conversations of the sort championed by the Cambridge Inter-Faith Programme led by Professor David Ford. Those conversations occur when people of different faiths read sacred scriptures together and discuss them from the perspective of their own beliefs. Reading books such as this one and engaging in those conversations will surely deepen a whole host of understandings about one's own traditions, as well as the traditions of others. Such conversations will promote respect and understanding about the world's major religions and show how faith is a powerful force for good in the modern world.

HE SHEIKH NAHAYAN MABARAK AL NAHAYAN
Minister of Culture, Youth and Community
Development, United Arab Emirates

PREFACE

I wrote *Jesus of Arabia* while living in the United Arab Emirates, and I originally envisioned it for readers in the Gulf region to better understand each other. But *Jesus of Arabia* has the potential to enhance understanding worldwide, far beyond the Gulf. Why should people outside the Gulf read this book? The simple answer is so that we can have a deeper knowledge and appreciation of Jesus.

It is fascinating to me, residing in the Middle East, that I have gained a better understanding of Jesus by being immersed in the Islamic culture of the Arabian Gulf. Let's be honest. Many people who don't live in Muslim-majority nations, whether they are Christian, secular, or of another faith tradition, are uncertain about Islam or afraid of what sometimes seems to be an alien faith. Even those who are well intentioned and try to seek meaningful encounters across faith traditions can quickly find obstacles and discouragement. Dialogue gets bogged down in theological dogma, the politics of terror seem to lurk just under the surface of conversation, and the gap between those of the Islamic faith and mainstream Western culture simply seems too wide to bridge. The result is a mentality which says "I will never get across this divide," which results in anything from apathy through to "I oppose this religion," which leads to hostility. Is there a middle way? How can we build a bridge between Christianity and Islam?

I believe the most important thing we have in common is Jesus. More specifically, the Jesus of Arabia. A Jesus who is both familiar and unfamiliar to Westerners and Arabs.

As an ordained Anglican priest, I've worked with the Church in the Middle East for more than two decades. I've lived in Turkey, Jordan, Kuwait, and now the United Arab Emirates. In all these countries I was a member of what was often a small Christian community. Most of my neighbours were Muslims, and every day I was exposed to the Islamic cultures of these different countries. I have spent numerous hours in conversations with Arab Muslims, and I have discovered something startling. They have a deep respect for Jesus, and they love him. My Muslim friends often light up when they talk about Jesus, and Christian friends are shocked by their interest and familiarity with Jesus. Christians are often unaware that Jesus is mentioned numerous times in the pages of Islamic scripture, the Holy Qur'an. Of course, Muslims have a different understanding about Jesus than Christians do, but they relate to Jesus because he is from the Middle East and because he is a revered prophet in the Qur'an. At first, I couldn't discern why there were many things in the Arab Islamic world which were oddly familiar. It took a while for the penny to drop, but eventually I realized the familiarity came from my knowledge of Jesus in the Gospels. His worldview and personality were profoundly shaped by living in the Middle East—and this worldview remains largely unchanged to this day.

I grew up believing Jesus was an Englishman. The blond-haired, blue-eyed pictures of Jesus used in my Sunday school reinforced the conviction that Jesus was like me. It was only after moving to the Middle East that the rather obvious truth hit me. The real Jesus was nothing like a European. He would have shared the dark complexion of his Middle Eastern contemporaries, and he spoke Aramaic and Hebrew, sister languages of Arabic. He had far more in common with my Muslim Emirati and Kuwaiti friends in his lifestyle than with me, an English Christian. Even so, it took me a while to see how that truth could help me to understand Islam in a way which respects and honours the many men and women who are just as devout as I am in seeking to know and follow God. Concentrating on the person of Jesus is one way to cross the divide between Christians and Muslims.

And I am not alone. In America there is a small but growing movement in which Christians and Muslims dedicated to an interfaith encounter which is centred on 'Simply Jesus'. This trend is becoming known to both Muslims and Christians who gather in arguably the most influential city in America: Washington, DC.

In 2017 I travelled to Washington, DC, to attend the National Prayer Breakfast. After two decades of living in the Middle East where daily life is infused with religion, I thought I was used to being surrounded by a public religious culture. Even so, nothing prepared me for the overt spirituality of this unique American event. Gathered in the same space were some of the most powerful politicians in the United States, including the president and the vice president, senators, congressmen and -women, senior leaders in the world of industry and business, political leaders of other nations, and faith leaders from all religions. What shocked me was that they were openly speaking of being gathered around the person of Jesus Christ. His life and teaching, his ethical thought and example proved to be the glue which brought diverse religious leaders into an atmosphere of prayer and respectful dialogue. The name of Jesus was spoken a lot, with warmth and conviction, and not just by Christians. This was a surprise.

Jesus of Arabia was written for two audiences. I wrote for Western Christians who do not know very much about Islam, and I wrote for my Muslim Arab friends who see the Christian faith as a Western imposition upon their world. For the latter I wanted to remind them that Jesus is a child of the Middle East, and that his message and culture may have far more resonance and meaning with them than it does for Western Christians. I wanted to connect these two worlds.

At a time when Islamophobia is on the rise in the United States and in Europe, there is a greater need than ever for Christians and Muslims to meet in the spirit of Jesus. To be gathered around the person of Jesus who modelled forgiveness, who taught the primacy of loving God and neighbour. Too much rhetoric from religious and political leaders accent the differences between Christianity and Islam. Those differences are real, and I address them in part 5, "The Elephant in the Room." But we cannot allow the differences to be the only focus of interfaith encounters. Looking at Jesus through the prism of doctrine, ecclesiology, and theological commentary has its place—but by their very nature, they tend to appeal only to specialists. Instead, the focus on *culture*, that word we use to describe the space in which human life is daily manifested, is instantly more accessible to all of us. Issues of etiquette, hospitality, gender roles, art, and poetry are all part of our human flourishing. This is what unites us. *Jesus of Arabia* reveals the world that Jesus inhabited, and a world which, in a real way, is still extant. We find it in the Islamic world of the Middle East.

Memories I took from the National Prayer Breakfast included a Muslim woman weeping as she shared her story of racial and religious abuse in America—often committed by those who would describe themselves as Christian. I remember being challenged by a Muslim, who after declaring his love for Jesus, wished that Christians would be more diligent in applying the teachings of Christ to their own lives. He cited Mahatma Gandhi of India, who expressed profound admiration for Jesus, and who when asked why he was not a Christian, replied "when Christians start following Christ then I shall consider becoming a Christian." Ouch!

So, how do we begin a dialogue with one another, without recriminations, misunderstanding, and accusations getting in the way? I suggest that a good place to begin is by looking at the person of Jesus afresh. To see him in the context of Middle East culture, that part of the world which seems so alien and frightening to many Americans. This is not a new approach. One of the great scholars who introduced a fresh understanding of the culture of Jesus is the outstanding American theologian, the late Kenneth Bailey, whose many works have been an inspiration to me as a pastor and a teacher. I am indebted to him and for the many insights which have enabled me to see more clearly the connections to my Western Christianity and the world of Islam. This book is my hopelessly inadequate tribute to him.

Jesus of Arabia is about respect. I deeply respect the religion of my Arab friends, and knowing and appreciating Islam has deepened my own faith. It is about cherishing Middle Eastern culture, because it is the culture of Jesus Christ. I want to retrieve the Jesus of history who through accident of modern imperialism and colonialism has become infused with a Western identity. In rediscovering Jesus as a Middle Easterner, I found transformation in my attitude to Muslim Arabs. In asking questions of Arabs about Jesus, in laying aside my Western presuppositions, I learn more about the one I have dedicated my life to following.

I want to gather friends to a banquet feast, and invite Muslims and Christians to engage once more with what Jesus actually said and seek mutual understanding and acceptance.

ACKNOWLEDGMENTS

T O A LOVING AND merciful God, who created the heavens and the earth – to You be glory and honour. To God who sent the prophets, and who sent Jesus to be Messiah, be praise and thanks. In Him I live, and move, and have my being.

I am blessed that I live in a country which proactively welcomes the Christian community. This hospitality flows out of a deep religious conviction embedded in Islam. This generosity of spirit is most clearly evident in the lives of the rulers of the United Arab Emirates and I am particularly grateful for the support of HE Sheikh Nahayan Mabarak Al Nahyan, the Minister of Culture, Youth and Community Development for the UAE.

St Andrew's Anglican Church in Abu Dhabi is a great place. They have encouraged me to be creative and explore new projects through which the church can engage with the wider community. For that I thank them.

The idea for this book began as a series of conversations for a video project with a film maker called Ray Haddad. Ray is one of the most creative people I know, and so I thank him for inspiring me and helping me to develop this concept.

I thank Teresa Penman for her excellent pencil sketches, which capture some of the iconic images of the Arabian

Gulf. Teresa has lived in the region for a long time and I cherish our friendship and times of shared ministry.

I also thank Bart Yarborough, Ethan Ebenezer, and Helen Verghese for going through the text and making helpful comments and insightful additions to the text. My thanks to Lisa Haddad too, for her excellent editing. My most savage editor was Malcolm Nelson and I thank him for taking on the task. To Pastor Cameron Arenson of the Evangelical Church in Abu Dhabi, I convey my gratitude for his willingness to check out the theological accuracy of my statements from a Biblical perspective. I remain as always in debt to Peter Hellyer who is unequalled in his knowledge of local Gulf culture. Much gratitude and thanks too to Pastor Jim Burgess of the Fellowship of the Emirates for his unstinting support and belief in this project.

I also want to thank the Motivate team. I have always appreciated Ian Fairservice's unrivalled enthusiasm and passion for all things Arabian. John Deykin has been a wonderful source of encouragement and is a raconteur par excellence. Thanks too to the very professional editor Poonam Ganglani, Victor Mingovits for his design genius, and to Emilie El Jaouhari for her tireless commitment to the business side of publishing. I feel truly honoured to be a part of the Motivate family.

A surprising source of encouragement came from my eleven-year-old daughter who read the script and helped me see things I had not seen before. For fun and stimulating conversations, thank you, Kathryn.

INTRODUCTION

W HERE DO WE BEGIN an interfaith dialogue between Muslims and Christians about Jesus?

I believe an important place to start is with the Gospels found in the New Testament. This is because the Christian values the Gospels as the authoritative source of information about Jesus, his words, and his works. There are also Islamic sources which speak of Jesus, not least the Holy Qur'an itself. These sources combined lead to a consensus between the faiths that Jesus was a historical figure who was defined as a prophet and teacher sent by God. Beyond that however, is a sharp division of opinion about Jesus. I want to look at some of the teachings and events of Jesus as outlined in the Gospels and explore how Middle Easterners and Arabs would have potentially interpreted them.

We start with an encounter recorded in Luke's Gospel between Jesus and a tax collector called Zaccheus.

AN ENCOUNTER WITH JESUS

Jesus entered Jericho and was passing through. A man was there by the name of Zaccheus; he was a chief tax collector and was wealthy. He wanted to see who Jesus

was, but because he was short he could not because of
the crowd. So he ran ahead and climbed a sycamore-fig
tree to see him, since Jesus was coming that way. When
Jesus reached the spot, he looked up and said to him,
'Zaccheus, come down immediately. I must stay at your
house today.

– Luke 19:1–5

This story in the Gospel of Luke goes on to record how
Zaccheus took Jesus home and demonstrated his repentance by returning ill-gotten excess taxes to the people he
had cheated. Meanwhile, the crowds muttered about the
poor choice of company Jesus was keeping.

The scandal of the story of Zaccheus, at least in the mind
of Western Christian readers, is that Jesus condescended
to spend time with a corrupt tax collector. As a tax collector,
Zaccheus was seen as a collaborator with the Roman forces
which occupied his community. As such, he would have
been regarded as a despicable traitor. This is a very familiar
story in the Western church, and the main point, as taught
by centuries of theologians, is that Jesus came to save sinners. There is really no other lesson which can be drawn
from this story. Or is there?

For a group of Omani readers encountering this story for
the first time, the story excited comment on other grounds.

'This is absolutely outrageous behaviour,' said one
Omani to the agreement of the others. 'How could Jesus
be so impudent to invite himself to another man's house!
In our culture we would not dream of inviting ourselves
into a neighbour's house unless we were explicitly invited
by the host. Not even the Sultan of Oman has the right to
walk into the most humble citizen's home – he must wait
to be invited. The only person who would have that privilege would be God himself.' His comments trailed off as he
realized the import of what he had just said.

Witnessing this dialogue was an American Christian scholar. Although he was an accomplished theologian, he had never before encountered such a novel interpretation of the story of Zaccheus. His encounter with the Omanis provoked a number of tantalizing questions regarding the meaning of this well-known Gospel story.

Steven Caton, an American anthropologist, records in his *Yemen Chronicle* a similar Arabian aversion to the idea of inviting oneself. He was told that it was considered *'aib'* (shameful) to visit the tribes uninvited.'[1]

SOME QUESTIONS

Has the Western Church missed the real point of the story all these centuries?

If the culture of Jesus resembles Gulf Arabian culture rather than that of the West, would Arabs have a better understanding of his message?

Would an Omani interpret this story differently from a Kuwaiti or a Bahraini?

The only way to find out would be to hear the reflections of Gulf Arabs as they read the Gospels and respond with their thoughts on how they interpret the meaning of Jesus' words and actions through the prism of their own culture.

Therein lies the rub. We will not find out what an authentic Gulf Arab interpretation of these stories might be unless they get the opportunity to encounter the teachings of Jesus. Traditionally this has been discouraged on the grounds that Orthodox Islam teaches that the Holy Qur'an should remain the only source of understanding the person of Jesus. Yet the Holy Qur'an itself advises Muslims to turn to the books of the Jews and Christians in order to confirm truth.

> If you doubt what We have revealed to you, ask those
> who have read the Scriptures before you. The truth has
> come to you from your Lord: therefore do not doubt it.
>
> – Sura 10:94

The most important question should be, 'What did Jesus actually say?'

Of all the questions that lie at the heart of interfaith dialogue between Christians and Muslims, perhaps this is the most essential one.

Muslims are convinced that the original message of Jesus has been changed or lost. They have come to this conclusion for a number of reasons. Firstly, the idea of a prophet claiming divine status is anathema to Islam.

Secondly, Muslims point to textual studies as evidence that the contents of the Gospels have not been preserved faithfully, and so consequently there is little confidence that we do have access to what Jesus actually said. They highlight that Jesus spoke in Aramaic, yet the earliest records we have of his teachings are in Greek. Has anything been lost in translation?

The four Gospels (Matthew, Mark, Luke and John) contain a lot of teachings of Jesus which are similar to each other. However, each Gospel also contains stories which are unique to the author of that particular gospel. They also have omissions or variations of the same stories which are found in the other Gospels. These observations have led Muslims to ask, 'How reliable are the Gospels in preserving the original message of Jesus?'

Then there is the question of interpretation.

Has the message of Jesus, as originally understood by a Middle Eastern audience, been changed as a result of having been filtered through a Western culture? As we have already seen before, Arabs had a very different take on a

Gospel story compared to the interpretation provided by the Western Church.

In order to understand Christian beliefs it is essential that we get back to the question of what Jesus actually said.

Christians believe that there are grounds for having confidence in the words of Jesus as recorded in the Gospels. The reasons for their confidence will be highlighted throughout this book. This confidence is based not on a forced or false article of faith but on a reasonable and empirical approach to the text of the Gospels as historical documents. At the end of the book, I document more fully some of the reasons why Christians have confidence in the veracity of the Gospel accounts and why Muslims can also have confidence in them too.

Next, if it is taken that the Gospels are a reliable account of Jesus' teachings and actions, how were they interpreted by his original audience in a Middle Eastern setting?

Exegesis is the discipline of 'reading out' of the sacred text the behaviour, culture, religion, and meanings of the world that Jesus inhabited at the time. Good exegesis therefore should lead to a reasonably accurate understanding of what Jesus was trying to communicate to his audience.

It is in this area of exegesis that interfaith dialogue between Christians and Muslims might yield fruitful insights. This is because the traditional cultural world of the Arab is much more in sync with the mindset of Jesus than a typical Western Christian.

In summary then, this book seeks to highlight those connections between the cultural world of Jesus with the Islamic cultural world of the Arabian Gulf. It takes as a starting point some selected teachings of Jesus as found in the Gospels and explores how they might have been interpreted in an Arabian context.

In writing this book I had two audiences in mind: the first is the expatriate Western Christian who lives in this region. Gulf Arabian culture reflects much which is familiar in the lands and culture of the Bible. The cultural similarities include the strong commitment to family life and tribal allegiances, and an understanding of shame and honour which permeated the peoples of the Scriptures. There are also connections with the physical geography of the Bible with reference to the sea, mountains, deserts and oasis.

I want to explain the culture of the Arabian Gulf to Western expatriates who may be completely unaware of the Biblical relevance of the surroundings in which they are immersed.

There are also many Christian expatriates in the Gulf who come from places like India and the Philippines. I am not specifically thinking of them as an audience for two reasons. One is that the Church in the East has a very different history from the Church in the West. This is especially so in their relationship with Islam. Islam in the West has always been defined in negative terms as the remote 'other', whereas in the East, Islam has been a much more immediate presence and by and large an integrated part of their history. As a direct consequence of this historical integration, the Church in the East is more able to connect culturally with the word of Jesus because they still live in cultures in which the Biblical cultural concepts of shame and honour still govern behaviour.

Secondly, there is a rich tradition of Bible commentary and scholarship in Asian languages which I cannot even begin to portray or access for the reader of this book.

So I write as a Western expatriate Christian, seeking to engage with the culture of the Arabian Gulf through the stories and teachings of Jesus Christ.

There is of course a danger in speaking of a 'Gulf Arabian culture'. The temptation is to see all Arab culture as a monolithic entity, but the fact is there are considerable differences between Arab cultures and apparent similarities are nuanced. These have been extensively mapped out by different authors who recorded regional differences in Arab history, opinion, and culture.[2]

It must be clear too that the culture in the Gulf is distinctive from other Middle Eastern cultures. Disappointment has been expressed by Gulf Arabs at the way their culture has been dismissed due to stereotypes:

> One view is that the Gulf is a backward region in which inadequate education, easy wealth, male dominance and tribalism have militated against cultural dynamism, so traditional cultural norms and practices persist. A contrasting view is that the region is super modern, with the rapid pace of globalization having thoroughly undermined traditional culture, replacing it with cosmopolitan, international one in which women are leading the way. A negative view which combines both these two opposites suggests that traditional culture has essentially been destroyed while a modern one has yet to take root.[3]

Yet the Arabian Gulf countries are regarded as part of the Middle East by virtue of their language, religion, and geographical connectedness. What separates the Gulf country from other Middle Eastern countries is undeniably the phenomenal 'rags to riches' story. This sudden wealth resulted from the discovery of abundant oil fields in their territories. The result was a massive flood of migrant labour, which poured into the region bringing the necessary manpower and skills to develop the new oil-fuelled economy. These distinctive accidents of history give the Arabian Gulf countries a different dynamic from other Middle Eastern countries, especially in the area of relating to people of non-Islamic faiths.

The second audience are the Gulf Arabs themselves.
Many of them will have had exposure to other cultures
through attending schools and colleges in the West. Many
will have lived with and worked alongside Christians from
all over the world. Yet there are many questions which puz-
zle them about Christian beliefs. Not least, there is a struggle to understand the Christian doctrine of Trinity and the
offensive idea that Christians believe in a God-Man. The
temptation is to dismiss Christianity as a corrupt 'Western'
religion which is far removed from the original message
of Jesus. I want to recapture for them the Middle Eastern
roots of a faith which the Qur'an itself testifies is a revelation of God to mankind. While the Qur'an mentions
Jesus and indeed reveres him, there is very little contained
within its pages about the contents of Jesus' teachings.
Geoffrey Parrinder in his book, *Jesus in the Qur'an*, sums
up the Qur'anic teachings about Jesus:

> He is a 'sign', a 'mercy', a 'witness' and an 'example'.
> He is called by his proper name Jesus, by the titles
> Messiah (Christ) and the Son of Mary, and by the names
> Messenger, Prophet, Servant, Word and Spirit of God.
> The Qur'an gives two accounts of the annunciation and
> birth of Jesus, and refers briefly to his teachings, healings,
> and his death and exaltation. Three chapters or suras
> of the Qur'an are named after references to Jesus
> (three, five, and nineteen[4]); he is mentioned in fifteen
> suras and ninety-three verses. Jesus is always spoken
> of in the Qur'an with reverence; there is no breath of
> criticism, for he is the Christ of God.[5]

There are several accounts of Jesus' teachings in Islamic
sources. These have been compiled together by Tarif
Khalidi in his comprehensive book, *The Muslim Jesus*,
on the sayings and stories of Jesus in Islamic literature.

However, the parables and teachings of Jesus are mainly recorded in the pages of the New Testament Gospels.

One huge problem which prevents Gulf Arabs from accessing the teachings of Jesus is the charge of *tahrif* (change or corruption) of the Gospel text. This perception of the unreliability of the Gospel text means that there is no confidence given to the historical integrity of the Gospels as a source of a faithful and true record of Jesus' teachings. Clearly, the Christian will need to demonstrate from a historical approach as to why anyone can take the Gospel accounts as trustworthy. This whole issue of *tahrif* will be discussed fully in Appendix A at the end of the book.

Western Christianity itself is now so far removed from the Semitic culture of the New Testament that Western Christians themselves are in danger of misunderstanding the social context of the teachings of Jesus. The Bible is a Middle Eastern book and it has a great deal to say which is still relevant to Middle Easterners today as well as the rest of the world. This is because it continues to address the universal themes of humanity, such as the need to find security and peace, an identity which defines our purpose, the desire for harmony between nations, peoples, and the environment.

In a time when Islam and Christianity are in danger of becoming more estranged from one another, it is hoped that this study of the teachings of Jesus will provide one facet of interfaith dialogue. It is an attempt to provide a tool of explanation and to make connections with that which is familiar between us.

THE CONTEXT FOR *JESUS OF ARABIA*

There are nearly 50 million people[6] in the region who might describe themselves as *Khaleeji;* that is someone who is a citizen of an Arabian Gulf country (*Khaleej* is the Arabic word for Gulf). I am pleased to count myself as living amongst them. I love living in the Gulf. Coming from the UK, I can honestly say that there is something wonderfully energizing about waking up daily to sunlight streaming through the bedroom window. The days of trudging to work in the dark and coming home in the dark while being battered by freezing, merciless rain seem wonderfully distant. Many exult in the amazing lifestyle on offer here. The superb shopping malls, the gleaming towers and dizzying architectural styles set a backdrop to daily life which can only be described as 'Hollywoodish'. Richard Poplak (2009), in his highly entertaining and revealing travelogue, *The Sheikh's Batmobile,* documents with some wonder the technological impact of American social media and highlights the sophisticated and modern tastes of Gulf Arabs. Globalization is writ large here. From the familiar brands of products through to mass produced media, there is always something somewhere in the Gulf which connects with the home of an expatriate. Another attraction is the sheer diversity of people who live here. According to figures which the Ministry of Labour released to *the Khaleej Times* on 25 August 2006, there are two hundred and forty-eight nation states in the world. Two hundred and two of those nations are represented in the Gulf.

In the excitement of all this glitz and glamour and the sheer exoticness of it all, it would be easy to overlook the timeless culture of the Gulf Arabs; a culture which pre-existed oil and the wealth it bought; a culture which is steeped in the soil of the desert land and centred around tribal identity and practice. I saw evidence of this culture as I moved around the Gulf in all sorts of places: a majlis[7] tent pitched in front of a home, a shepherd boy calling sheep out of my suburban garden, a wedding dance performed on wasteland next to a villa, a banquet for complete strangers held in a tent in front of a shopping mall. As I became aware of this culture, I was startled to discover that it was not as alien as I assumed it would be. It seemed somehow familiar and eventually I made the connection. The resonance I felt with the Arab culture in the Gulf was rooted in my faith as a Christian. The world of the Bible, its cultures and traditions were all being mirrored in the living tradition of the *Khaleeji* Arabs.

I suddenly found that the teachings of Jesus came to life in the context in which I was living. I had several 'Aha!' moments when I recognized behaviour which was clearly familiar to the original listeners of the Gospel stories. This is what has provoked me to write this book about the teachings of Jesus.

SO IS THIS JUST ANOTHER BOOK ABOUT JESUS?

There have been a great many books written about Jesus Christ of Nazareth. Some are controversial, others are conservative. Jesus has been portrayed over the years as a wandering sufi-like mystic, a hippy who sought inspiration from magic mushrooms, a cunning political conspirator, a Jewish sage, or even a myth. In his most recent book, *Zealot: The Life and Times of Jesus of Nazareth*, Iranian Muslim author, Reza Aslan, posits that the 'real' Christ of history was a political rebel who was executed by the Romans on the charge of treason.

Let me state at the outset what this book is not about.

It is not a narrative or a reconstruction of the Jesus of orthodox Christian faith or history (I happen to believe they are both the same).[8]

It must also be said that this book is not an apologetic for the Christian faith, nor is it a manual aiming to 'convert' people to my point of view.

This book is written to spark a conversation, a dialogue about what Jesus means to both Christians and Arab Muslims. It is written in order to explore the common ground between the faiths using Arabian Gulf culture as a mediator.

BIBLICAL CULTURE AND ARABIAN CULTURE

A valid question to ask would be, 'Is the Biblical culture similar to the culture of the Arabs in the Gulf?' Certainly there are some big differences. The New Testament setting is during a time of occupation by the Roman Empire when Greek was the *lingua franca* of the ancient world, although the local language in which Jesus spoke and taught was Aramaic. The Jewish faith and community feature largely in the narratives surrounding Jesus, and the majority of the population were settled in villages and towns, unlike the perceived nomadic lifestyle of the Arabs. The religious landscape was varied with pagan cults and temples visibly endorsed by the Roman Empire. It seems a world apart from the Arabian Peninsula.

However, there is much that connects the world of the Bible with the culture of the Arabian Gulf.

To start with is the shared Semitic origins of Middle Eastern languages. It is easy to forget that Jesus spoke in Aramaic due to the fact that the earliest surviving written records of his teachings were in Greek. The New Testament Greek narrative masks the powerful Semitic oratory style of Jesus which has its equivalence in the Arabic language. It is worth noting that the Mel Gibson movie about the trial and execution of Jesus, *The Passion of the Christ,* was understood by Arabic audiences, even though the whole screen play was performed in Aramaic. They are sister languages drawing on the same structure, roots and a shared world view.

Secondly, the popular perception that the inhabitants of Arabia are all nomadic is false. A substantial part of the population dwelled in villages and towns and the Arabian Gulf is no exception. Writing about the Trucial States (so called because of the treaty the British made with the tribal leaders) which is now the UAE, Donald Hawley observes that the population:

> ...are divided into two classical Arab categories, the *Hadhr* and the *Bedu*. The *Hadhr* are the settled people living in the towns and the gardens of the eastern mountain area and the oasis. The *Bedu* are the nomadic people of the desert, and the timeless struggle between Cain the cultivator and Abel the shepherd is re-fought annually when *Bedu* animals stray into the gardens.[9]

Thirdly, the geography of the Bible reflects the landscape and sometimes the actual places of the Arabian Gulf. The physical environment one lives in shapes cultural behaviour. Thus the lifestyle of the nomad and villagers dwelling on the edge of the desert will find parallels across the centuries from Biblical times to the present. One example of this is the culture of hospitality found across the Middle East. Below is a Biblical example.

HOSPITALITY

> Abraham looked up and saw three men standing nearby. When he saw them, he hurried from the entrance of his tent to meet them and bowed low to the ground. He said, 'If I have found favour in your

eyes, my lord, do not pass your servant by. Let a little
water be brought, and then you may all wash your feet
and rest under this tree. Let me get you something
to eat, so you can be refreshed and go on your
way – now that you have come to your servant.

– Genesis 18:2–5

As we can see Abraham exemplifies the hospitality of
the Arabian Peninsula. Abraham has travelled with his
family from what is now Southern Iraq and is resting by
his tent. Then he sees the strangers and immediately offers
them hospitality. He instructs his wife Sarah to bake some
bread and then sacrifices a calf and prepares it for them as
a meal.

We see this code of hospitality still at work. It is rooted
in the harsh environment of the desert where a stranger
can approach a Bedouin encampment and, once accepted,
can be expected to receive hospitality for up to three days.
Hospitality is an expression of a family's honour and the
failure to provide it results in shame. Stories abound of the
generosity of Bedouin who gave their last livestock to be eaten
by complete strangers. Whilst this generosity can result in
poverty, the Bedouin' reputation of honour is secured.

DEFINING GULF ARABIAN CULTURE

In the Gulf region, former British diplomat Mark Allen[10]
highlights in his book, *Arabs,* some of the essential
components of Arabian culture and describes them as
the *jizz* of the Arab. *Jizz* is an ornithological term, which
describes the overall characteristics of a bird species thus
allowing it to be identified. He identifies four specific *jizz*.

He highlights the themes of 'blood' (the importance of tribe and family, shame and honour, and hospitality), religion (and how it shapes communities and serves as law), the defined and prescribed role of women, and finally the language – how the Arabic language acts as a central identity marker and guardian of tradition. The discerning reader will realize that these categories are generic and can be applied to many cultures around the world.

However, in deciding on a structure for this book I have decided to take these four defining *jizz* categories or essential components of the Arab spirit and try to relate the teachings of Jesus to them. This is a very artificial way of grouping the teachings of Jesus, and in fact several of Jesus' parables address more than one aspect of culture. Yet this is a useful tool to order and highlight the connection between Arabian Gulf culture and the teachings of Jesus. Therefore each section will begin with a more detailed look at the four *jizz* identified above and then the teachings of Jesus will be introduced in relation to that category.

As this is essentially a religious dialogue, it is important that we recognize the role of Islam in the Arabian Gulf. To talk about Arabian Gulf culture without reference to Islam would be like describing a marriage without reference to a husband or wife.

Let us be clear then that the most central aspect of Gulf Arabian culture is the religion of Islam. Life before Islam is documented through archaeological sites that reveal traces of an ancient trading people who lived in the Gulf for the past 4,000 years, and in some areas, even longer.[11] However, the pre-Islamic culture has been subsumed over the centuries into the fabric and worldview of Islam. Official statistics for virtually every Gulf Co-operative Council (GCC)[12] country reveal that the local population is 99.9 per cent Muslim. The only slight variation would be Kuwait and

Bahrain who have Christian, Baha'i, and even Jewish elements in their native populations.

THE ELEPHANT IN THE ROOM

Jesus was a child of the Middle East and he had far more in common with a Muslim Gulf Arab, in terms of culture and experiencing religious law, than with an American or British Christian (I have added the word 'with' because I am assuming that the reader will compare Jesus' culture with that of Muslims vs. Americans/the British, rather than comparing Muslims with Jesus and Americans/the British). Reclaiming this Jesus is one of the purposes of this book. I want to introduce the Christ of Arabia to people who live in the Arabian Peninsula.

There is much that Christians and Muslims have in common and I will highlight these points of connection throughout the text. I am conscious too of the sensitive theological issues separating Muslims and Christians and I have reflected on how to address these differences. The temptation is to ignore them altogether as discussion of these subjects usually ends up at an impasse and an atmosphere that is usually less than cordial. Nonetheless, to not acknowledge and attempt to explore the differences would only serve to ignore the 'elephant in the room' and leave the reader feeling dissatisfaction that those areas were not addressed. The subjects include the questions of the Trinity, the integrity of the Bible, the identity of Jesus and the events of his death. These are addressed at the end of the book under the title of 'The Elephant in the Room'. I have tried to be fair in my coverage of these key areas and avoided polemical language. I hope my presentation of the Islamic view is one which a Muslim will concur is a fair representation of their beliefs.

SOME DEFINITIONS

The word 'Gospel' refers to the content of the teachings of Jesus Christ preserved in the pages of the New Testament. 'Gospel' literally means good news and embraces not just the teachings of Jesus, but also his actions and his life, including his death and resurrection.

The most comprehensive definition of 'Culture' I have found is from the work of the scholar and missionary to India, Leslie Newbiggin. In his book, *Foolishness to the Greeks: Culture and the Gospel in Western Culture,* he explains that:

> By the word culture we have to understand the sum total of ways of living developed by a group of human beings and handed on from generation to generation. Central to culture is language. The language of a people provides the means by which they express their way of perceiving things and of coping with them. Around that centre one would have to group their visual and musical arts, their technologies, their law, and their social and political organization. And one must also include in culture, and as fundamental to any culture, a set of beliefs, experiences, and practices that seek to grasp and express the ultimate nature of things, that which gives shape and meaning to life, that which claims final loyalty. This includes religion.[13]

Applying this definition of culture to Biblical studies means that we can examine how the meanings and expressions of contemporary life compare and contrast with those found in the pages of scripture. One scholar who excelled in applying cultural insights from the New Testament is Dr Kenneth Bailey.

A MODEL OF CULTURAL ANALYSIS

I am indebted to the work of Dr Kenneth Bailey who unpacked the cultural background of the New Testament, thus opening fresh and new ways of understanding the Scriptures. Kenneth Bailey lived in the Middle East for sixty years. He spent his childhood in Egypt and spent forty years teaching the New Testament in seminaries in Cyprus, Lebanon, Jerusalem, and Egypt. He dedicated his academic career to understanding the teachings of Jesus through the cultural framework of the Middle East. To accomplish this, he used two approaches. The first being ancient, medieval and modern oriental sources. Through these writings of Middle Eastern scholars he would glean fresh insights into how they interpreted the teachings of Jesus. In particular, he is 'convinced that the Arabic Bible has the longest, most illustrious history of any language tradition'[14].

The second approach was to conduct extensive interviews among Levantine and Egyptian villagers, especially the older generation who are still tapped into an oral tradition. He would ask questions along the lines of, 'How would your grandfather have understood this teaching of Jesus?' In doing so, he would capture memories of a lifestyle and interpretation that was not far removed from that of villagers who lived at the time of Jesus.[15]

The conclusion of this book suggests that the next step of our dialogue is to explore doing a cultural study of the Gospels specifically in an Arabian Gulf context using the tools developed by Dr Bailey. An alternative tool is the use of Scripture Reasoning between resident expatriate Christians and Gulf Arabs, and this is introduced at the end of the book.

---

1   Steven Caton, *Yemen Chronicle: An Anthropology of War and* Mediation (New York: Hill & Wang, 2005), p. 50.
2   See for example the work of James Zogby, Kenneth Cragg, Hourani, A. 1991 and Phillip Hitti.

3   Reported in Alanoud Alsharekh & Robert Springborg, *Popular Culture and Political Identity in the Arab Gulf States* (London: SOAS, 2008), pp. 9–10.

4   The suras are respectively named 'The Family of Imran', 'The Table', and 'Mary'

5   Geoffrey Parrinder, *Jesus in the Qur'an* (London: Faber, 1965), p. 16.

6   http://www.arabianbusiness.com/gcc-population-will-near-50m-by-2013-445943. html. Accessed 9 April 2014.

7   Majlis is an Arabic word meaning 'meeting place'.

8   I define the orthodox understanding of Jesus as that expressed in the words of the Nicene Creed. This was a historically defining statement produced in AD 325 in which the early Church Bishops settled competing views about the nature of Christ.

9   Donald Hawley, *The Trucial States* (London: Allen & Unwin, 1970), p. 22.

10 Mark Allen worked for the British Foreign Service in the Middle East for more than 30 years. His first posting was in Abu Dhabi where his keen interest in falconry led to a good rapport with Sheikh Zayed.

11 See for example see the works of Jehan Rajab, Peter Hellyer & Dr Michele Ziolkowski, and Timothy Insoll.

12 The Gulf Co-operation Council (GCC) was founded in 1981 and includes six countries: Bahrain, Kuwait, Qatar, Oman, Saudi Arabia and the United Arab Emirates.

13 Lesslie Newbiggin, *Foolishness to the Greeks: The Gospel and Western Culture* (Michigan: Eerdmans Publishing Company, 1986), p. 3.

14 Kenneth Bailey, *Who are the Christians in the Middle East?* (Michigan: Eerdmans, 2008), p. 13.

15 Two of his publications in particular have been pivotal, they are *Poet and Peasant and Through Peasant Eyes* and *Jesus through Middle Eastern Eyes*. For a more scholarly and comprehensive approach on this whole area of Middle Eastern culture in the Bible I unreservedly refer the reader to these two books.

PART ONE
FAMILY, HONOUR AND HOSPITALITY

OVERVIEW

I and my brother against my cousins
I and my cousins against the outsider[1]

THE ROLES OF TRIBE and family are an essential part of life in the Arabian Peninsula. This is defined by Mark Allen as one of the essential components of the Arab spirit. Blood ties define the status and identity of Arab individuals. Coming from a culture in the West where individualism is revered as a core value, it may be surprising to realize that it is seen as a weakness in the East. Making important decisions is seen as the domain of the elders and leaders of the family and tribe. I remember seeing this most clearly during parliamentary elections in Kuwait. The tribes would forward their family members as candidates and instruct their families to vote for them. The political system of Kuwait depends on the tribes voting for their kinfolk en bloc. Family members are raised to think of themselves as 'we' (belonging to a family) rather than 'I'. This is one of the distinctive facets of Gulf Arabs. Margaret Nydell, an expert in Arab culture and language, drives this point home:

> *Family loyalty and obligations take precedence over loyalty to friends or the demands of a job.* Relatives are

expected to help each other, including giving financial
assistance if required... Only the most rash or foolhardy
person would risk being censured or disowned by
his or her family. Family support is indispensable
in an unpredictable world; the family is a person's
ultimate refuge.[2]

THE BIRTH OF JESUS

Belonging to a family meant Jesus had obligations and a
clear role. In the eyes of his community, Jesus was in fact,
defined by his family. They defined his social status, education,
religion, and occupation. This is unsurprising, as
Middle Eastern behaviour revolves largely around family
life. In this matter Jesus was typical of the time and place
in which he was born.

On another level it is safe to say that the account of
Jesus' birth is unusual. The Gospel records a miraculous
birth in which Jesus is born to the young Mary as a result of
a promise from Gabriel, a messenger of God. The Gospel
of Luke tells the story as follows:

> In the sixth month of Elizabeth's pregnancy, God sent
> the angel Gabriel to Nazareth, a town in Galilee, to a
> virgin pledged to be married to a man named Joseph,
> a descendant of David. The virgin's name was Mary.
> The angel went to her and said, 'Greetings, you who
> are highly favoured! The Lord is with you.'
>
> Mary was greatly troubled at his words and wondered
> what kind of greeting this might be. But the angel said to
> her, 'Do not be afraid, Mary, you have found favour with
> God. You will conceive and give birth to a son, and you
> are to call him Jesus. He will be great and will be called

the Son of the Most High. The Lord God will give him the
throne of his father David, and he will reign over Jacob's
descendants for ever; his kingdom will never end.'

'How will this be,' Mary asked the angel, 'since I am
a virgin?'

The angel answered, 'The Holy Spirit will come on you,
and the power of the Most High will overshadow you.
So the Holy One to be born will be called the Son of God.'

– Luke 1:26–35

There is a mild debate among linguists over the Greek
word used by Luke to describe Mary as a virgin. Some who
have difficulty in coming to terms with the idea of a 'virgin
birth' find that an alternative meaning for this Greek word
is 'young woman', which they argue does not necessarily
imply virginity. This point is moot given that Mary clearly
understood the facts of life when she asked the angel how
she could have given birth without losing her virginity. The
mystery of how Jesus was conceived is described in language that conveys God's role in bringing or willing the
child into existence. This is clearly emphasized when Jesus
is first described as 'the Son of God' in the Gospel.

It is understandable then that the Prophet Muhammad,
who grew up in a pre-Islamic environment where pagan
legends were rife with the sexual antics of gods begetting
other deities through carnal means, would interpret this
story as another disappointing pagan myth. The title, 'Son
of God', would conjure up associations of a male deity producing offspring by copulating with a female deity. This
was just too much for the Prophet, who held God (Allah)[3]
in supreme reverence. God would not descend to the level
of the lusty pagan gods. This would imply then that there

were other beings who were equal to God (Allah) and this would violate a core conviction of Islam, namely, that God is One. There is nothing like Him, and to associate another being or object with the same status or identity would be to commit the grave sin of *shirk* (association with God). In actual fact, the Christian would be in agreement with the distaste felt by the Prophet, as Jesus is believed by Christians to be the result of a divine creative action of God's Holy Spirit.

People are surprised to learn then, that in the light of the Islamic discomfort with Jesus being described as a 'Son of God', that Muslims also believe Jesus was the result of a virgin birth. It must be stressed though that despite belief in the virgin birth, Muslims do not believe that Jesus is the 'Son of God' in any shape or form.

It is fascinating to read this testimony of the virgin birth recorded in the Qur'an:

And you shall recount in the Book the story of Mary: how she left her people and betook herself to a solitary place to the east. We sent to her Our spirit in the semblance of a full-grown man. And when she saw him she said; 'May the merciful defend me from you! If you fear the Lord, leave me and go your way.'

'I am but your Lord's emissary,' he replied, 'and have come to give you a holy son.'

'How shall I bear a child,' she answered, 'when I have neither been touched by any man nor ever been unchaste?'

'Thus did your Lord speak,' he replied. 'That is easy for me. He shall be a sign to mankind and a blessing from Ourself. Our decree shall come to pass.'

Thereupon she conceived him, and retired to a far off
place. And when she felt the throes of childbirth she lay
down by the trunk of a palm tree, crying: 'Oh, would that
I had died before this and passed into oblivion!'

Carrying the child she came to her people, who said to
her, 'Mary, this is a strange thing, Sister of Aaron. Your
father was never a whore-monger, nor was your mother
a harlot.' She made a sign to them pointing to the child.
But they replied, 'How can we speak with a babe in
the cradle?'

Whereupon he spoke and said, 'I am the servant of God.
He has given me the Book and ordained me a prophet.
His blessing is upon me wherever I go, and he has
exhorted me to be steadfast in prayer and to give alms as
long as I live. He has exhorted me to honour my mother
and has purged me of vanity and wickedness. Blessed
was I on the day that I was born, and blessed I shall be on
the day of my death and on the day I shall be raised to life.'

Such was Jesus son of Mary. That is the whole truth,
which they still doubt. God forbid it that He Himself
should beget a son! When He decrees a thing He need
only say: 'Be,' and it is.
                                          – Sura 19.16–23 and 27–34

In essence then, the Holy Qur'an agrees with the Gospels
that Jesus' birth was a unique event in that there was a direct
intervention by God in producing a baby within Mary. In
some interpretations of the Qur'an, the villagers come out
to confront Mary because she has brought dishonour to
their community by having a child out of wedlock. The only
thing that saved her from an 'honour' killing was that Jesus
spoke from the cradle. It is therefore significant that the

Qur'an refers to Jesus as the 'Son of Mary' because Arab tradition normally identifies the male child as the progeny of the father. Typically, Jesus should have been described as the son of Joseph (Ibn Yusuf). Jesus is therefore perceived as a product of a virgin birth, with God acknowledged as the initiator. What the Qur'an is quick to deny, is that this birth is the result of a sexual liaison. God, in his role as creator simply speaks life into being. By uttering a word, his will is manifested physically in the world. This idea is not unique to Islam. The Genesis account of creation begins with God speaking the world into existence:

> And God said, 'Let there be light,' and there was light.
>
> – Genesis 1:3

Muslims and Christians are therefore united in the belief that the birth of Jesus was an act of God. Some other comments can also be made about this passage. There is the brief statement about the infant Jesus blessing the day of his birth, death, and raising up, which some read as an Islamic prophecy of his death on the cross and subsequent resurrection. Scholars point out that a similar statement from John the Baptist is also included in the Qur'an; he used the identical benediction for himself.

THE FAMILY OF JESUS

Two of the Gospels (Matthew and Luke) list the genealogy of Jesus' family. Much has been made of the differences between the two lists but the differences are accounted for by the fact that Matthew traces the lineage through Joseph in order to establish Jesus' family credentials for a Jewish, patriarchal readership, whereas Luke traces the genealogy through the line of Mary and in doing so highlights a reverence of Christ for his gentile readers. Both genealogies make it clear that Jesus belonged to a specific tribe and family (the House of David), which rooted him in time and place. The significance of the House of David is that it is a kingly line and that many of the Old Testament prophecies relate to a descendant of David as ushering in a new era.

The unusual circumstances of Jesus' birth were not lost on Joseph who was betrothed to Mary at the time she was pregnant. As a Middle Eastern man, this brought huge shame on his family and on Mary in particular. He was a decent man and decided to guard the family honour:

> Because Joseph her husband was faithful to the law, and yet did not want to expose her to public disgrace, he had in mind to divorce her quietly.
>
> – Matthew 1:19

That Joseph did not divorce Mary is due to the explanation in scripture that an angel convinced him to look after Mary and the child.[4]

After Jesus was born, Mary and Joseph went on to have other children. The Gospels recorded that Jesus had brothers and sisters[5] and that the community referred to him as the son of Joseph, the carpenter.[6] Jesus seems to have been aware that he was somehow different from the rest of the family, even as a child. The only childhood story the Gospels record is the one in which Jesus visits Jerusalem with his family on pilgrimage. Jesus is twelve years old and in the midst of the crowds he becomes separated from his family. Mary and Joseph spend three days frantically searching for him, finally finding him in the temple, listening to the teachers of religion. After being rebuked by his parents, Jesus said, 'Why were you searching for me? Didn't you know I had to be in my Father's house?' (Luke 2:49).

One of the most controversial stories concerning Jesus and his family sees him dismissing his family and placing the mission of God above them:

> While Jesus was still talking to the crowd, his mother and his brothers stood outside, wanting to speak to him. Someone told him, 'Your mother and brothers are standing outside, wanting to speak to you.'
>
> He replied to him, 'Who is my mother, and who are my brothers?' Pointing to his disciples, he said, 'Here are my mother and my brothers. For whoever does the will of my Father in heaven is my brother and sister and mother.
>
> – Matthew 12:46–50

This would have been an unthinkable thing for a Middle Easterner to say, undermining the first loyalty that everyone in his society would have shared – family. These words would have deeply wounded his immediate family and would have been seen as a betrayal. However, Jesus was clear in his teaching that the Kingdom of God took priority for him and his followers. Family obligations could not be used as an excuse for not serving God and His Kingdom.

It is worth noting that Joseph is absent from this event and that there is no reference to him as father. Scholars have suggested that by this time Mary was a widow.

From that moment on there is no more mention of Jesus' father in the Gospels, thus reinforcing the idea that Joseph died prematurely, leaving Jesus as the oldest son to provide for his brothers and sisters and mother. As the firstborn son it was his sacred duty to ensure that he provided for the family, ensure that his sisters were married, and that his brothers were established in the family trade.

Finally, he had to bury his parents with due dignity and honour. Only then would the firstborn son fulfil his duties.

That Jesus started his ministry so late in his life (it is understood that he began preaching at thirty years of age), indicates that he waited until he had fulfilled his duties as the firstborn son in his family. His final duty of providing for Mary into her old age is poignantly recorded when he hands over that responsibility to one of his close disciples as he is dying on the cross:

> When Jesus saw his mother there, and the disciple whom he loved standing nearby, he said to her, 'Woman, here is your son,' and to the disciple, 'Here is your mother.' From that time on, this disciple took her into his home.

> – John 19:26–7

Only then, after he had discharged all his duties as a family member, did Jesus lay down his life.

---

1   Gina Benesh, Culture Shock. *A Survival Guide to Customs and Etiquette. United Arab Emirates* (New York: Marshall Canvendish, 2008), p. 75.
2   Margaret Nydell, *Understanding Arabs: A Guide for Westerners*, (Maine: Intercultural Press, 2002), p. 91.
3   Allah is an Arabic word simply meaning the God. There has been much debate about whether Allah is the same God described in the Bible. For a full discussion on this issue I refer the reader to Miroslav Volf's work, *Allah: A Christian response*.
4   Matthew 1:20–25
5   Luke 2:7
6   Luke 4:22, Mark 6:3

CAMEL

It is easier for a camel to go through the eye of a needle
than for someone who is rich to enter the Kingdom of God.

– Mark 10:25

For those that have denied and scorned Our revelations
the gates of heaven will not be opened; nor shall they enter
paradise which will be as impossible as the passing of a
camel through the eye of needle.

– Sura 7.40

Do they never reflect on the camels, and how they
were created?

– Sura 88.17

I T IS HARD TO imagine a camel beauty contest. I had never heard of such things until I came to the Arabian Gulf,
but they really exist! It is a measure of the deep affection
that the Arabs have for these 'ships of the desert' that they
find them aesthetically pleasing as well as essential for survival in the harsh desert environment.

Camels are fascinating creatures. They are uniquely
adapted to the desert. They do not pant or sweat but instead
have an internal thermostat, which raises their normal

body temperature in accordance with the external climate heat and in this way conserve body fluids. No other animal can do this. Camel hair is extremely effective as an insulator from the heat. While the surface temperatures may reach seventy degrees Celsius the actual skin temperature of the camel is thirty degrees Celsius lower. Cutting the hair of a camel can lead to a fifty per cent increase in water loss.

When it comes to diet, the camel's digestive system is ideally suited to the sparse vegetation found in desert environs. Ahmed Al Mansoori, a renowned Emirati scholar, marvels at how well adapted the camel is to the desert:

> Its highly mobile upper lip is split and this enables the animal to eat rough, thorny bushes without damaging the lining of its mouth. Its lower lip is suspended. It can gather food without the help of the tongue, which therefore loses no moisture. A camel gulps down its food without chewing it first, later regurgitating the undigested food and chewing it in cud form. The camel's food is pushed back and forth through four stomach chambers, which extract nourishment from the unlikely sources with very little waste. The animal has very dry dung that burns well for cooking.[1]

The earliest mention of camels in literature is in the Bible. In the Genesis accounts of Abraham we read that during his time in Egypt the Pharaoh owned, among other things, camels.[2] Abraham sent his slave by camel to look for a wife[3] and they feature in stories about Jacob[4] and Joseph.[5] Camels were also used in warfare.[6] The Priestly code laid out in the book of Leviticus forbids the worshippers to eat camel because 'they do not have a cloven hoof' (Leviticus 11:4). Ahmed Al Mansoori summarizes the presence of the camel in the Bible.

Camels in the Old Testament are mentioned on most
occasions in which the 'people of the East' or the Arabs
are referred to. They appear in the account of the Queen
of Sheba, and in that of Job, who had three thousand
camels when he died. The first book of Chronicles gives
an account where 50,000 camels were plundered in a
single raid.[7]

The most striking thing about the camel for the newcomer is its size. When one sits on the back of an adult
camel the ground seems awfully far away. Camels not only
carried people but were beasts of burden used to trans-
port everything from water through to market goods. Fully
laden, a camel could fill a substantial space. So the notion
of a camel going through the eye of a needle becomes even
more absurd and comedic in the mind of the hearer who
knows how massive these animals are.

In Mark's Gospel (10:17–27), we read that a young ruler – a
wealthy and religious young man – approaches Jesus and
flatters him by addressing him as 'good teacher'. Normally,
in Middle Eastern culture flowery rhetoric indicates good
education and manners, and a suitable response to flattery is
to return it. Thus the young ruler may have been expecting
Jesus to respond with reciprocal flattery, saying something
along the line of 'Noble ruler' or 'Esteemed Leader of men'.

Jesus does none of that and would have come across as
rude and abrupt. Instead of playing the game and flattering
the ego of the wealthy young man, Jesus throws a challenging question at him: 'Why do you call me good? Only God
is good'.

Then Jesus goes on to make his comment about the
camel going through the eye of a needle. If taken literally,
Jesus is saying to this rich young ruler that it is impossible for him to enter the Kingdom of God. You can almost
see the followers of Jesus slapping themselves on the head

as Jesus dismisses what could have been a very promising candidate for their cause. He had money, he had influence – the sort of person any organization would have been delighted to have on board. Instead Jesus practically insults him, effectively declaring him a lost cause.

Over the years, commentators have tried to soften this saying by looking for alternative meanings or allegories in the hope of rescuing the harshness of Jesus' response. After all, Church leaders do not want all rich and powerful people to feel that Jesus is prejudiced against them!

The following explanations have been offered, leaving room for an interpretation that offers some hope to those who do find comfort in their materialistic wealth and influence.

THE CAMEL IS NOT A CAMEL

The word camel did not refer to the beast of burden; it was a word referring to a thin rope. This is a very old attempt and involves changing a vowel in the Greek text of the New Testament. Kenneth Bailey explains:

> Instead of reading *kamelon*, if we read *kamilon* (as some ancient manuscripts give us) we are not talking about a large, four-legged animal, but rather a rope. Thus if you imagine a thin rope and large enough needle, it becomes difficult but not impossible for the rope to be pulled through the needle. The implication then is that it is just about possible for a rich man to get into the kingdom of God.[8]

This explanation is rejected, however, for being unconvincing and slight. As far back as the eleventh century,

Ibn Al Tayyib, an Arab Bible commentator, dismissed this interpretation:

> Some say that the word camel in the text means a thick rope. Others think that it is a large beam that provides support for the foundation of the roof, and others say that it simply means the well-known animal; and this is the correct opinion.[9]

THE CAMEL IS A DOOR

Another suggestion is that the eye of the needle refers to the small door built into the large, heavy gates, which frame the entrance to a compound or city. Usually, the twin doors are made of heavy beams, which require much effort in opening. So for normal use, a smaller door allows access for the visitor. The idea, then, is that a fully loaded camel would normally walk through a wide open door, but sometimes an unloaded camel might be squeezed through the small cut-out entrance without recourse to swinging open the double gates.

F. W. Farrar quotes private correspondence recollecting travels in the Middle East in 1835 in which the traveller did find a door called the needle's eye.[10] This idea was completely dismissed by Bailey and Scherer, who are both long-term residents in the Middle East, and have never heard of the smaller door set in large gates being described as the 'eye of a needle'.[11]

Another theory was that the eye of a needle described a small gap in the walls of Jerusalem. When the main gates of the walled city were closed, latecomers could enter into the city through this small entrance. If they had pack animals with them, they would have to laboriously unload them in order to take them through the eye of a needle. Needless to say, there is no archaeological evidence to suggest such an entrance through the walls of Jerusalem existed.

The inescapable conclusion then is that Jesus really meant a camel. The story is a literal example of something, which is quite impossible. A huge beast cannot go through the eye of a needle, and in the same way, rich men cannot enter heaven simply because they are rich.

This is a shocking thing to say in Middle Eastern society. There is a simple test of finding out if a man has favour in God's eyes or not. The evidence is in his health and wealth and prosperity. As Bailey said, the mentality would have been:

> Rich men are able to build places of worship, endow
> orphanages, offer alms to the poor, refurbish temples,
> and fund many other worthwhile efforts. If anyone is
> saved, surely it is they. Jesus says that such people cannot
> enter the kingdom by such noble efforts. We commoners
> do not have the wealth to carry out such noble deeds.
> Who then can be saved?[12]

The listeners of Jesus would have assumed that the more prosperous you are, the more righteous you are, as God rewards the deeds of good people. In essence, Jesus said to the young man, 'Don't put your trust in your riches.' Our material possessions have no meaning in the eyes of God. Instead, he looks for hearts that are 'contrite and humble' (Psalm 51).

The people who were most amazed were the disciples. Peter finally said, 'Lord, we have left everything to follow you' (Mark 10:28), to which Jesus replied:

> No one who has left home, or brothers or sisters or
> mother or father or children or fields for me and the

Gospel will fail to receive a hundred times as much in
this present age.

— Mark 10:29–30

What is striking about Jesus' response to Peter is that he
lists the primary duty of the Middle Easterner as being loyal
to family and property. The disciples would have felt these
pressures keenly. The teachings of Jesus directly challenge
these loyalties. Bailey explains:

> It is no mistake that 'house' occurs first on the list of
> specifics. Members of the family then make up the other
> four items in the list of five. This leads to a comparison
> of the old and new requirements of religious obedience.
>
> In the old obedience the faithful were told not to
> steal another's property. In the new obedience, one's
> own property may have to be left behind. In the old
> obedience one was told to leave the neighbour's
> wife alone. In the new obedience the disciple may
> be required to leave his own wife alone. In the old
> obedience the faithful were to honour father and mother,
> which of course properly understood, meant (and still
> means) to stay home and take care of them until they
> die and are respectfully buried. In the new obedience
> the disciple may have to leave them in response to a
> higher loyalty. It is nearly impossible to communicate
> what all of this means in our Middle Eastern context.
> The two unassailable loyalties that any Middle Easterner
> is required to consider more important than life itself
> are family and the tribal village home. When Jesus puts
> both of these in the same list and then demands a
> loyalty that supersedes them both, he is requiring that
> which is truly impossible to a Middle Easterner, given
> the pressures of his culture.[13]

The conservative Gulf Arab would equally be scandalized by this teaching, as family and tribal loyalties are the
primary values which govern their behaviour. Their reaction would mirror that of Jesus' original Middle Eastern
audience, whose shocked reaction would have been, 'This
is impossible!'

---

1   Ahmed Al Mansoori, *The Distinctive Arab Heritage: A Study of Society, Culture and Sport
    in UAE*. (Abu Dhabi: Emirates Heritage Club, 2004), p. 59.
2   Genesis 16:10
3   Genesis 24: 10–17
4   Genesis 30:43
5   Genesis 37:25
6   Judges 7:12, 8:21
7   Al Mansoori, pp. 38–39.
8   Kenneth Bailey, *Poet & Peasant and Through Peasant Eyes*. (Michigan: Eerdmans,
    1983), p. 165.
9   Ibid. p. 166.
10 Farrar, F. W. 1876. 'Brief Notes on Passages of the Gospel. II. The Camel and the
    Needle's Eye'. *The Expositor* (First Series), Vol. 3. pp. 369–80.
11 Bailey, p. 166.
12 Ibid. p. 167.
13 Ibid. p. 169.

MAJLIS

When he noticed how the guests picked the places of honour at the table, he told them this parable: 'When someone invites you to a wedding feast, do not take the place of honour, for a person more distinguished than you may have been invited. If so, the host who invited both of you will come and say to you, "Give this man your seat." Then, humiliated, you will have to take the least important place. But when you are invited, take the lowest place, so that when your host comes, he will say to you, "Friend, move up to a better place." Then you will be honoured in the presence of all the other guests. For all those who exalt themselves will be humbled, and those who humble themselves will be exalted.'

– Luke 14:7–11

MANY TRADITIONAL ARAB HOMES will have a room designated solely for hospitality. These are usually located at the front of the house with a separate entrance so that men visiting will not disturb the women of the house. The Majlis is simply a meeting room where men gather to talk through issues of the day and just to spend time with one another.

Once inside the Majlis, the custom is to greet the host who usually sits in the centre of the room furthest away from the door. As you approach the host he will stand and all the guests will stand as one. After you have greeted the host, you then shake hands with all the guests going around the room in a circle. If this is a large Majlis with up to a hundred men gathered, this can take time. With a steady stream of visitors you feel as if you spend most of the time standing, waiting to shake hands with yet another guest who is working his way round the room.

THE DILEMMA

The awkward part of this ceremony is knowing where to sit after greeting everyone. There is usually an unspoken hierarchy, which determines the seating arrangements. The rule is simple. The more important you are to the host, the closer you sit to him. It's not just about social ranking, though I have noticed on more formal occasions the Arabs very quickly sort out their seating arrangements according to status. Family often esteem their guests by pushing them closer to the host. Modest Arabs will go out of their way to ensure that another guest sits closer to the Sheikh. Consequently, there is a great deal of shuffling as people shift positions in order to accommodate newcomers.

Sometimes it is clear. If someone of higher status than the host arrives, then the host indicates this by moving forward to greet him in the middle of the room, escorting him back to his seat, and making sure that the guest sits immediately to his left or right. Generally the right hand side indicates the higher status and favour of the guest. (I always think of the Nicene Creed, which describes Jesus as sitting at the right hand of the father).

So what do you do if there is no direction from the host as to where you sit? The desire of the visitor is usually to have some interaction with the host, and the easiest way to have a conversation with him is to sit close. However, that might mean displacing someone who the host really wants to talk to. Therein lies the dilemma. It is in addressing this dilemma that the words of Jesus in the Gospel of Luke have proven to be of enduring relevance.

There was (and still is) a similar practice at the time of Jesus in the village communities of Palestine. Those who have least rank sit by the door, and those regarded as elders of the group sit near the centre. A sort of visible demotion takes place when a guest is asked to sit nearer the door. Of course for most people this is simply the ebb and flow of the Majlis. After you have spoken to the host and he wants to speak to a newcomer, you slide out of the way, satisfied with your encounter. Problems arise when someone feels snubbed or thinks they are entitled to a favoured seat without invitation. I have seen this happen and I confess that if a guest is clearly being pompous or presumptuous, there is a small sense of satisfaction in seeing him asked to readjust his perceived status.

THE DILEMMA SOLVED

In a culture where one of the markers of your social status can be indicated, literally, by where you sit, the potential for humiliation (no matter how unintended) is high. The advice Jesus gives to his Middle Eastern audience is simple and telling.

He is saying to them, 'Swallow your pride, seek humility, and always sit by the door!' His logic is impeccable. If you really have any status in the gathering, then straight away the host will notice you and bid you to move up. In this way a guest is honoured and 'promoted' before the presence of all the other guests. This is very affirming.

So, following the advice of Jesus, I head towards the door, and often I hear the host calling my name and inviting me to sit somewhere else. If I don't hear my name, I sit by the door anyway, and I know my place.

Going to a Majlis is one of the most interesting activities an expatriate can engage in. It is amazing who you meet and a fascinating place for learning about culture and history. Over the years, I have met artists, poets, pop stars, politicians, corporate business leaders, sporting personalities, and heads of nations and royalty. Yet the weekly dilemma for those new to the Majlis remains: 'Where do I sit?'

As always with the teachings of Jesus, there is a hidden layer of wisdom, which the discerning listener would have picked up on. On the surface, this story seems to contain good advice as to how one resolves the dilemma of where you sit when you go to visit your host. Be humble and you will be honoured, if you are seen worthy of it. Otherwise, you run the risk of being dishonoured in front of the guests, and that really does not feel too good. 'Everyone who exalts himself will be humbled, and he who humbles himself will be exalted' is how Jesus sums up his lesson. There is another dimension though, and this is easily missed.

Closely linked with this story of the feast is the important parable of the Wedding banquet; this is the subject of the next chapter.

WEDDING

T'S NOT JUST THE Majlis where seating is important. The same protocol plays out at meals, banquets, and feasts. This is not so unusual to Westerners. After all, at wedding receptions in the UK we have our head table where the significant parties involved in the wedding are expected to sit. I mention weddings because the gathering Jesus is talking about in the story previously discussed is a wedding feast. His observations of proud people sitting in the most favoured seats prompted his teaching on this matter. However, this is not simply a lesson on morals or behavioural etiquette. There is a religious dimension to this story, and the clue lies in the fact that it is a wedding feast.

A wedding in any culture is usually a big deal, but Middle Easterners really take this to a whole new level of celebration. It is a great excuse for extravagance and for bringing everyone together. Of course, there is also the opportunity to preen and establish one's social status in front of the whole community. It is this behaviour that Jesus zooms in on, and he highlights a real spiritual danger, which we will come to later on.

Dr Mary was a medical doctor in Arabia during the pre-oil era. She describes a wedding she attended in Kuwait:

We arrived in the evening. The street in front of the house was full of black-cloaked women trying to get in. The gatekeeper was supposed to admit the invited and keep out the gatecrashers. The poor man could not identify veiled women, so the crowd smothered him. We had to push our way into the open courtyard where about a hundred women were sitting on mats being served with sweet drinks and biscuits.

Umm Abdullah took us to see the bride who was sitting alone on the floor of a small dark room saying her prayers. She had heavy gold jewelry, a headpiece of one inch gold squares joined together in a block and set with turquoise and cornelian, necklaces, rings, bracelets, a nose ring, pendants in her long black hair. She was the picture of Oriental splendor. We were then taken to see the bridal chamber. It was one of the best rooms of the house. The couple could occupy it for the first seven days of the marriage receiving callers. After that the bride would be taken to the home of her mother-in-law which would then become her home. We sat in the courtyard to await the coming of the bridegroom. As in Jesus' story of the ten virgins he tarried a long time – two hours in fact. Finally there came a cry, 'Here's the bridegroom!' and the young man appeared.

On the wedding day the men attend the mosque for evening prayers and then after an all men's gathering they come to the bride's house where the men of the bride's family welcome them with congratulations. An incense pot wafting fragrant frankincense is passed around. Silver rosewater shaker perfume the guests clothes. Bitter, hot coffee, flavoured with cardamom is served by male servants. Then all the men depart, and the father of the bride escorts the groom to the bridal

chamber, where he awaits his bride. The women bring her,
veiled, and present her to the groom. The next morning
evidence of the bride's virginity is displayed to the family.[1]

One of the best accounts of a contemporary Emirati
wedding is found in the book, *Mother without a Mask*.[2] The
author, Patricia Holton, describes in detail the days of preparation and ritual that go into a tribal wedding. She details
the interactions between the men and the women, the lavish food preparation and the atmosphere of excitement.

At the time of Jesus, weddings were no different. The
families of the bride and bridegroom would come together
with the whole community to celebrate the union over several days of feasting and ritual. Sometimes the wedding
feast was hijacked by a more odious agenda. Great store
is set by the wedding's invitees and honour is given to the
families if a noted personality shows up. Some things have
not changed in the Middle East over two thousand years.
In the newspapers of the Gulf, there are frequent reports
and photographs of weddings, and they place great emphasis on the guests. The principle is the same. A wedding can
become a showcase for the status of the family.

Jesus talks about weddings a lot. In fact, the first miracle he ever performed in public (according to the Gospel
of John) was at a village wedding feast in Cana. There is
a reason why he refers to weddings in his storytelling and
events. The reason is that in the Old Testament, or the
Torah, wedding feasts and banquets were a sign of the coming of the Kingdom of God, and those who were invited
were those upon whom God's favour rested.[3]

The wedding banquet, thus, is a familiar metaphor for
the religious people in the Middle East, meaning that those
who are favoured by God will be blessed by being in his
presence as a perpetual guest. A common saying at the
time of Jesus was, 'Blessed is he who will eat at the feast of

the Kingdom of God'. It was a way of saying, 'I am a religious person and close with God!'

In this parable of the feast, Jesus is addressing a very religious audience. He is speaking to learned scholars and rabbis who have literally spent years studying their sacred scriptures. Their piety was absolute and was exhibited through the strict ritual and regular worship, which marked the life of a devout God-fearer.

American author and pastor, Rob Bell, describes the formation of religious leaders at the time of Jesus:

> Their education would have begun at the age of six in the local synagogue and they would have been taught by a local rabbi. This first level of education was called *Bet Sefer* (which means 'House of the Book') and lasted until the student was about ten years old. By the age of ten years, gifted students would have memorized the Torah by heart.
>
> Rabbis who taught the Scriptures were the most respected members of the community. They were the best of the best. They were the smartest students. Not everybody could become a Rabbi.
>
> By the age of ten years, students who showed promise went onto the next stage of learning called *Bet Talmud* ('House of Learning') and this lasted until they were around the age of fourteen years. During this time they would memorize the rest of the books in the Scriptures.
>
> Finally, at the age of fourteen or fifteen years, the brightest students would then approach a Rabbi and ask to be his disciple. This stage of learning is called Bet Midrash ('House of Study') and they would commit to not just acquiring the knowledge of the Rabbi, but also

the way he lived and they would imitate his religious
discipline. The amount of learning is phenomenal.
Eventually they may get to the stage where they start
their own teaching ministry around the age of thirty.[4]

The formation of religious leaders in the Middle East
really has not changed much since the time of Jesus.
Muslim students are encouraged to memorize the Qur'an
from an early age, and I have met several children who
were 'hafiz' (someone who has memorized the Qur'an
completely) by the time they were ten years old. To continue in Islamic education, the student is then introduced
to the world of commentaries (known as *Tafsir*) and begins
to study the schools of Islam and religious jurisprudence
(*Fiqh*). Again, a good student is expected to memorize
the works of the classical scholars and to be able to apply
this knowledge in their own teaching and understanding
of their faith. Islamic scholars and religious leaders are
therefore people who have been processed through years
of training.

In short, the religious leaders listening to Jesus knew
their religion. They had memorized vast chunks of
Scripture and were intimately acquainted with the commentaries and studies surrounding their sacred texts. They
would know that the symbol of a banquet would mean a
discussion about God being present with his people. They
would have instantly picked up on the hidden meaning
Jesus was conveying through his story. And it would have
made them very angry.

HUMILITY

In his lampooning of the haughty wedding guests who
were trying for the best seats, Jesus was making a telling

criticism of the religious attitudes of the leaders of his community. In virtually all the wedding metaphors in the Scriptures, the host of the wedding nearly always refers to God himself. The banquet was a code picture used by the people to refer to the time when God would take his people to paradise – to be in the presence of God Himself.

The point Jesus is making in this story is that humility is important to God. Too often the religious leaders were quick to make assumptions and create a theology, which might lead to a sense of superiority or self-righteousness. He likened the religious leaders to those arrogant guests who assumed high status at the wedding feast only to be humbled by the host (usually understood to represent God). Jesus appears to argue that favour in the eyes of God depends not on religious knowledge or practice, but rather a spirit of humility. The same spirit that drives a guest who has no status to sit by the door is the spirit that results in God exalting the guest in the presence of everyone.

The hard-hitting message of Jesus to his religious audience then is simply this: without an attitude of humility, we simply cannot know God.

The Parable of the Great Banquet narrates the following:

> When one of those at the table with him heard this, he said to Jesus, 'Blessed is the one who will eat at the feast in the Kingdom of God.' Jesus replied: 'A certain man was preparing a great banquet and invited many guests. At the time of the banquet he sent his servant to tell those who had been invited, "Come, for everything is now ready." But they all alike began to make excuses. The first said, "I have just bought a field, and I must go and see it. Please excuse me." Another said, "I have just bought five yoke of oxen, and I'm on my way to try them out. Please excuse me." Still another said, "I just got married, so I can't come." The servant came back and reported this to

his master. Then the owner of the house became angry
and ordered his servant, "Go out quickly into the streets
and alleys of the town and bring in the poor, the crippled,
the blind and the lame." "Sir", the servant said, "what
you ordered has been done, but there is still room." Then
the master told his servant, "Go out into the roads and
country lanes and compel them to come in, so that my
house will be full.'"

— Luke 14:15–23

One of Jesus' most shocking stories concerning a wedding is when he tells the parable of a King who invites
selected guests to attend his wedding feast. As was the
practice in those days, the servants were sent out two or
three days before the event to invite the guests and then on
the day itself the servants would again be sent out to advise
the guests that the feast was now ready.

Can you imagine the insult to the King's honour when
his guests failed to turn up? The excuses they sent back
with the servants included, 'I've just bought a field and
I need to go and see it', or, 'I've just bought some oxen
and I am going to try them out', or, 'I've just got married'.
They were all shockingly insulting. As a Westerner reading
this, it seemed at first glance that these were reasonable
excuses, I could not really understand the significance of
these answers.

Kenneth Bailey highlights why the excuses were such
bad manners.

The first excuse was, 'I've just bought a field and I need
to go and look at it.' In a desert climate, arable land was at a
premium and no farmer would buy a piece of land without
seeing it and studying it over months to see how much yield
he would get from his potential crops. He would be intimately acquainted with the land before he parted with hard
earned cash for it. Bailey said it would be the equivalent to

'a Westerner who calls his wife to tell her that he will be late for supper because he has just purchased a new house over the phone and having signed the cheque now wants to drive across town to look at it!'[5] Such an excuse is highly implausible. The excuse offered by the first guest does not even pretend to mask the fact that he is simply snubbing the host of the banquet.

The second excuse is again a parody. The guest explains to the servant that he has bought oxen and now he needs to try them out. Again this would be an expensive and careful purchase that a farmer would have investigated thoroughly before purchase. Oxen need to work together as a team, and an unequally yoked pair pulling a plough leads to disastrous results. Oxen need to be compared for gait, speed, and size. This excuse was a public insult to the host of the banquet.

The final excuse is unbearably coarse: 'I have just got married'. Sex was and is a deeply taboo subject. Conservative religious Middle Easterners consider it crass, and the height of bad manners is to speak of sexual matters in public. The crude sexual reference given to the servant was deeply offensive, as it would be today. The servant would have blanched at such an excuse.

So the servant returns with a heart of shame. All the guests have united together to insult and reject the hospitality of their host. What will the King do? Such a snub would send anyone into a rage.

The King is entitled to be outraged by these insults. Hospitality then, as now in the Middle East, is a sacred duty. You show great honour to your hosts by attending their meals. To not show up, and even worse, insult your hosts, especially in front of the servants, would not go down well with Gulf Arabs. The consequences could be dire. At the very least, it would lead to a permanent disruption in the relationships between the King and his guests.

At worst, most neighbours would feel that he had justification to defend his honour by resorting to violence.

Instead, the King does something completely unexpected. He turns the deadly insults into an opportunity for grace to abound. The guests who were entitled to attend the banquet were pushed aside, and instead, the invitation was extended to a completely marginalized and neglected group. People who would never have dreamed of getting inside a palace, or who would never have expected to attend such a grand banquet were now being summoned.

The King reacts to the snubs of his original guests by inviting the most socially disadvantaged people in their community. Instead of raging at the insults, he transforms his emotional energies into grace. The servants were sent out to bring in the poor, the crippled, the blind, and the lame. Can you imagine a wedding story in *Gulf News* or *Arab Times* highlighting those kinds of guests? Again, there is a theological dimension to the description of the guests. At the time of Jesus, there was a group of devout religious men who asserted that there were some, who would be unable to enjoy the banquet of God: 'The one who is smitten in his flesh, or paralysed in his hands or feet, or lame, or deaf, or blind, or dumb, or smitten in his flesh with a visible blemish.'[6] These are the very ones who Jesus is now saying benefit from an invitation from the King.

Jesus was challenging the religious leaders of the day about everything they thought they knew about the Kingdom of God. They knew they were special, they had worked incredibly hard to earn their learning and their status, and they were proud of their religion. The lesson Jesus was conveying was that in the midst of their religiosity they had lost sight of something fundamental: humility. This attitude makes us approach God with a sense of awe and an awareness of our own inadequacy. This attitude allows us to recognize that we never stop learning. There are always new things to learn, new treasures to discover, new depths of knowledge to plunge. The pride of the religious leaders and their book knowledge had blinded them and even enabled them to distort the teachings of Scripture into something completely alien. The great prophet Isaiah foretold a day when, '... the Lord Almighty will prepare a feast of rich food for all peoples, a banquet of aged wine – the best of meats and the finest of wines.' (Isaiah 25:6) The banquet portrayed in this vision was inclusive of all peoples.

So the message is crystal clear. God's grace will be extended to all kinds of people. Even those who do not 'fit' the model of what is regarded as an appropriate religious, qualified person will be invited. God will not be exclusive.

There is one final twist in this story of the great banquet. It is the challenge to religious people who want to please God to be completely radical in their approach to hosting meals. The parable of Jesus has the King (understood to be God) extending his invitation to the banquet to those who cannot possibly reciprocate the invitation. Jesus challenges them to do the same. Will anyone dare to follow Jesus' advice about the wedding guest list when he says:

> When you give a luncheon or dinner, do not invite your friends, your brothers or sisters, your relatives, or your rich neighbours; if you do, they may invite you back and so you will be repaid. But when you give a banquet, invite the poor, the crippled, the lame the blind, and you will be blessed. Although they cannot repay you, you will be repaid at the resurrection of the righteous.

> – Luke 14:12–14

I did read about one couple who literally put this into practice. Bill Johnson writes about an American couple who prepared for their wedding by asking friends and family to provide them with 'coats, hats, gloves and sleeping bags' – to be given to their *guests*. After their wedding they went to the reception hall which was filled with the poor and the homeless and 'got behind the serving table, and dished the food for their guests. The meal was excellent and the hungry became satisfied'.[7]

It struck me during one Ramadan, when living in the UAE, that I saw a manifestation of this teaching to invite people to a feast with no reciprocation required. It was displayed through the presence of the *Iftar* tents that had sprung up around the city. These tents had been erected by companies or wealthy individuals who in turn sponsored the meals of anyone who came to the tent. Sometimes hundreds of labourers turn up to *Iftar* tents and enjoy the hospitality of their hosts, knowing that there are no strings attached – no money required, no conditions imposed in order to enter the tent. The meal is free and available.

This is a cultural tradition found in the Islamic world, which captures a core divine truth. This practice of charitable hospitality echoes the grace of God as taught by Jesus. Grace is given freely. We do not deserve it, we have not earned it, and our only possible response is humility.

1   Mary Bruins Allison, *Doctor Mary in Arabia* (Austin: University of Texas Press, 1994), pp. 50–52.
2   Patricia Holton, *Mother Without a Mask* (London: Kyle Cathie Limited, 1991), Chapters 15–19.
3   Isaiah 61.10, Isaiah 62.5
4   Rob Bell, *Velvet Elvis: Repainting the Christian Faith* (Michigan: Zondervan, 2005), pp. 126–131.
5   Kenneth Bailey, *Jesus Through Middle Eastern Eyes: Cultural Studies in the Gospels* (London: SPCK, 2008), p. 315.
6   Andrei Dupont-Sommer, *The Essene Writings from Qumran* (USA: Peter Smith Publisher Inc., 1973), pp. 107–108.
7   Johnson, B. *When Heaven Invades Earth*, (Shippensburg: Destiny Image Publishers, 2003), pp. 25–26.

PART TWO
RELIGION

OVERVIEW

THE SECOND ESSENTIAL COMPONENT of the Arab spirit, described by Mark Allen, is the role of religion. Islam has defined the Arab world since the seventh century. It is the basis of law and entwined in every aspect of Arab culture, from family life through to business. It is difficult to separate Islamic culture from the religion, for they are as thoroughly mixed as coffee in a cup of hot water. Islam is a distinctive world faith in that it stands apart from other religions with salient doctrines on the Unity of God and a scripture, which forms the basis for communal law. It is worth highlighting the core beliefs in Islam and examining how it is related to the faith and culture of Jesus. Many Christians do not have a good understanding of Islam and are therefore not able to see the connections between the world of the Bible and the Muslim world. I seek to provide a fair and accurate description of Islam to which my Muslim friends will be able to say, 'Yes! That is my faith'.

Islam is a religion of revelation. It does not claim human origin, but rather that God initiated the revelation of a book through an Arab man who was a devout believer. His name was Muhammad.

THE PROPHET MUHAMMAD

The Prophet Muhammad (PBUH)[1] was a merchant and a devout monotheist who sought solitude in the desert when seeking God. One day, while meditating in a cave, he heard a voice speaking to him, commanding him to recite what he heard. This was the pivotal moment when he became a prophet of Allah – an Arabic word which effectively acts as a proper noun literally meaning 'The God'.

With the support and encouragement of his faithful wife Khadijah, the new prophet began to challenge his kinsmen in the Quraishi tribe. The main religion of his local community at the time was based on a cube-like structure (the *Kaaba*), which housed 365 idolatrous representations of various gods and deities. Thus the Meccan tribe of the Al Quraish, the guardians of an animistic, cultic centre of pilgrimage, were challenged directly by Muhammad (PBUH) to turn from their pagan ways and worship the One God who is the Creator and Lord of Heaven and Earth.

Initially his message did not go down well, not least because he challenged the economic *raison d'etre* of his whole community. Slowly, he began to gather a community of believers around him who were persecuted by the local community for their new faith. The accelerating persecution in Mecca (pronounced *Makkah* in Arabic) necessitated the flight of the fledgling Muslim community to an oasis town across the desert called Medina. This flight (*Hijrah*) from Mecca to Medina marks the beginning of the Islamic calendar and the birth of the Islamic community.

It was in Medina where Islam emerged and flourished as a cohesive faith, which ultimately united the feuding desert tribes and led to the retaking of Mecca. Under the leadership of the prophet, Islam spread with astonishing speed across the Arabian Peninsula. Within three hundred years of Muhammad's death, the Muslims ruled an empire, which spread from Iran to North Africa and from Turkey down to Yemen.

Underpinning this vast empire was the Islamic creed (*shahada*): 'There is but one God, and Muhammad is His Messenger'. Each Muslim is supposed to fulfil the pillars of his faith by praying five times a day (*salat*), giving alms (*zakat*), observing the fast of Ramadan (*sawm*), and making the pilgrimage to Mecca (*hajj*) at least once in his or her lifetime. The literal root of Islam means submission. The word peace (*salaam*) also belongs to the etymological root family of Islam. We can conclude from the etymology then that Islam promises peace to the believer through submission to Allah.

Alongside the five pillars, Muslims express their belief in the religious doctrines of Islam. The most prominent belief is in the doctrine of the Oneness of God (*tawhid*), belief in the prophetic lineage starting with Adam going through to Muhammad (PBUH) who is the 'Seal of the Prophets' and thus the final recipient of divine revelation. Earlier revelations given to Moses, David, and Jesus are acknowledged as divinely authenticated. Angels feature largely in the spiritual cosmos of Islam, including *Jibriil* (Gabriel) who is used by Allah as a messenger. Islamic eschatology[2] warns of a judgment day in which non-believers are cast into a fiery hell, while the pious and devout will be admitted into paradise, which is portrayed as a luxuriant and sensuous garden.

Holding the community together is *sharia* law, which is the application of the Holy Qur'an, and a collection of the sayings of Prophet Muhammad (PBUH) called the *hadith*. *Sharia* law advises the community in every aspect of life, ranging from worship to warfare, and from family matters to commercial transactions.

It is clear that from the outset Islam was not just a religious belief system, but a whole means of governance.

The faithful are called to live under the dictates of divine law, and there was no distinction made between the temporal realm and a spiritual realm. In other words, the DNA of Islam contains the blueprint to be heaven on earth. The prospect of being a minority faith is alien to the logic of the Qur'an and hadith. Thus, according to Islam, the will of God is for all humans to be in submission. Peace on earth will only be accomplished if society obeys His will as revealed primarily in the Qur'an.

The link between Islam, Judaism, and Christianity is the shared conviction that God created the heavens and the earth and that He communicated with humans through his prophets. The Qur'an acknowledges the legacy of Biblical prophets and in particular sees a likeness between Moses and Muhammad who both received a divine law, which served to define their own community as distinct from 'others'. Both men were religious leaders, jurists, community leaders, statesmen, and military commanders. Both men were involved in leading a refugee people across the wilderness, and they both saw a miraculous expansion of their faith communities.

Reza Aslan argued that the Prophet saw his own ministry in the light of the earlier revelations to Jews and Christians, to the extent that he believed the Holy Qur'an was a continuation of one divine scripture revealed to the Jews and the Christians, and that they also constituted one divine community.

> As far as Muhammad was concerned, the Jews and
> the Christians were 'People of the Book', spiritual
> cousins who, as opposed to the pagans and polytheists
> of Arabia, worshipped the same God, read the same
> scriptures, and shared the same moral values as his
> Muslim community. Although each faith comprised its
> own distinct religious community (its own individual

Ummah[3]), together they formed one united Ummah,
an extraordinary idea that Mohammed Bamyeh called
'monotheistic pluralism'. Thus the Qur'an promises
that 'all those who believe – the Jews, the Sabians, the
Christians – *anyone who believes in God and the last days*,
and who does good deeds, will have nothing to fear or
regret' (5:69, emphasis added).[4]

One example supporting Reza Aslan's statement comes
from a well-attested Hadith found in the Bukhari collection:

My similitude in comparison with the other prophets
before me, is that of a man who has built a house nicely
and beautifully, except for a place of one brick in a corner.
The people go about it and wonder at its beauty, but say:
'Would that this brick be put in its place!' So I am that
brick, and I am the last of the Prophets.

– Sahih Al Bukhari 1:735

The laws the prophet revealed to the people governed
every aspect of life, and at the heart of it all was a liturgy
of worship towards God. It was to a Middle Eastern society
living under Mosaic law that Jesus came with his message.
The context in which he spoke would be a familiar one: a
community that was profoundly religious, led by learned
scholars who interpreted sacred Scriptures for the rest of
society, advising them on everything from the proper way
to pray through to personal hygiene matters and on how to
deal with the minutiae of daily life. Jesus quoted the Law
and the Prophets in his teachings and was intimate with
the challenges of living a life under religious law. His audiences consisted of settled villagers as well as nomads. They
came from all walks of life ranging from the farmer to the
fisherman, from soldiers to scholars. Women and children

were not exempt from his gaze, and they were included in his teachings and his travels. In short, Jesus spoke to a society, which was not so different from the communities of the Arabian Gulf today.

---

1   PBUH (Peace Be Upon Him) is a respectful salutation to all prophets of Islam.
2   A theological term referring to the study of the end of time.
3   Ummah refers to the concept of a 'people of God' who transcends nationality or race but are united by faith in God.
4   Reza Aslan, *No god but God. The Origins, Evolution, and Future of Islam.* (New York: Random House, 2011), p. 101.

FASTING

FASTING IS ONE OF the central pillars of Islamic beliefs and spirituality. During the holy month of Ramadan, millions of Muslims put themselves through a challenging period of fasting from sunrise to sunset, and the fast is total – no food, no liquids, no smoking, and no intimate relations. They are restricted to eating between sunset and sunrise. For some, this means a reversal of their daily routine. They sleep more in the daytime and stay up longer through the night.

For many Muslims, fasting is a discipline that has spiritual benefits. They are not the only ones who do this. In the time of Jesus, Jews, especially the Pharisees, fasted as a way of expressing their commitment to God. A devout Jew was expected to fast at least once a week. The Pharisees encouraged fasting up to three times a week. They were not shy about letting others know how spiritual they were. They would deliberately dishevel their clothes and look weak and pale in order to let others know that they were putting their bodies through a vigorous spiritual discipline.

Jesus fasted. He clearly saw it as a core spiritual discipline and implicitly expected his disciples to do the same. His ministry began with a forty day fast in the wilderness and his instructions to his followers were:

> When you fast, do not look somber as the hypocrites
> do, for they disfigure their faces to show others they are
> fasting. Truly I tell you, they have received their reward
> in full. But when you fast, put oil on your head and wash
> your face, so that it will not be obvious to others that
> you are fasting, but only to your Father, who is unseen;
> and your Father, who sees what is done in secret, will
> reward you.
>
> – Matthew 6:16–18

What does Jesus mean when he says that the men who broadcast their fasting publicly will get their reward? I think it simply means that the main reason why they publicly 'show off' their fasting is so that they can impress others with their discipline and commitment. If that is their goal, said Jesus, then they will be rewarded with acknowledgment and affirmation from those watching them. Their status and reputation among their peer group, for whom fasting is seen as a mark of spirituality will surely increase, but that is all. For those who fast in secret, however, Jesus promises something else. Their reward will not be respect and admiration from other men, but instead they 'will receive a reward from their Father in heaven' (Matthew 6:16–18).

Fasting is something of a lost tradition in the Western church. Islam, though, seems to have faithfully preserved some of the spiritual traditions of the early church. Perhaps this is not so surprising, for as William Dalrymple, a seasoned Scottish journalist and author who has travelled extensively throughout the Middle Eastern region, observes:

> Islam grew up in the largely Christian environment
> of the Late Antique Levant, and the longer you spend
> in the ancient Christian communities of India and
> the Middle East, the more you become aware of the

extent to which Eastern Christian practice formed
the template for what were to become the basic
conventions of Islam. The Muslim form of prayer with
its bowing and prostrating appears to derive from the
older Syrian Orthodox tradition that is still practiced in
pew-less churches across the Levant. The architecture
of the earliest minarets which are square rather than
round, unmistakably derive from the church towers of
Byzantine Syria, while Ramadan, at first sight one of
the most distinctive of Islamic practices, bears startling
similarities to Lent in which the Eastern Christian
churches still involved – as it once used to in the
West – a gruelling all day fast.¹

Clearly, saints through the ages testify to the power of
fasting. Fasting focuses our minds and our appetites. The
struggle to re-orientate our desires in the direction of God
reaps a spiritual depth and awareness, which is usually
clouded out by our daily mundane needs. But the danger is
that we use fasting to impress others and, even more fool-
ishly, to try and impress God.

There is another kind of fast, which the Scripture refers
to, one that seeks to address the problems mentioned above:

'Why have we fasted,' they say, 'and you have not seen
it? Why have we humbled ourselves, and you have not
noticed?' Yet on the day of your fasting you do as you
please and exploit all your workers. Your fasting ends
in quarrelling and strife, and in striking each other
with wicked fists. You cannot fast as you do today and
expect your voice to be heard on high. Is this the kind
of fast I have chosen, only a day for people to humble
themselves? Is it only for bowing one's head like a reed
and for lying in sackcloth and ashes? Is that what you
call a fast, a day acceptable to the LORD?

> Is not this the kind of fasting I have chosen: to loosen
> the chains of injustice and untie the cords of the yoke,
> to set the oppressed free and break every yoke? Is it not
> to share your food with the hungry and to provide the
> poor wanderer with shelter – when you see the naked,
> to clothe them, and not to turn away from your own
> flesh and blood?
>
> — Isaiah 58:3–7

Is this a kind of fasting that can be shared by Muslim and Christian? There is a fascinating trend in interfaith relations labelled as 'co-belligerent theology'. The premise of this collaboration is that both Islam and Christianity have common theological resources, which can inform and motivate both communities to combat universal social foes, such as poverty or human trafficking. Thus, fasting is both about being close to God and being concerned about social justice.

Jesus clearly identifies his own fast with the above Old Testament passage by publicly reading out a passage from scripture and linking it with his own divine mission. He proclaimed that the Spirit of the Lord was upon him and that he had been given a mandate to bring the good news to the poor, to heal the sick and to set free the prisoner. This was in stark contrast to a joyless and stern application of religious law, which felt more like a punitive measure rather than bringing heaven on earth.

In a religious society, the discipline of fasting can degenerate into a mechanical exercise in which the letter of the law is met, and it becomes a grim race between members of the community to fulfil their obligations. Despite this potential danger for legalism, Jesus never implied that fasting in and of itself was bad. He was critical of people who were religious hypocrites because in the process of being mechanically devout they disconnected themselves from the spiritual obligation of meeting the needs of their fellow human beings. According to Jesus then, the purpose of fasting is that it brings us close to God, and as a consequence, this fasting produces compassion. The thrust of Jesus' teaching then can be summarized in the following words: When a religion becomes devoid of compassion, then that religion has become estranged from God.

1   William Dalrymple, *From the Holy Mountain: A Journey among the Christians of the Middle East* (London: Holt Paperbacks, 1999), p. 105.

PEARL

Again, the kingdom of heaven is like a merchant looking for
fine pearls. When he found one of great value, he went away
and sold everything he had and bought it.

– Matthew 13:45–46

O NE THING I ALWAYS associate with the Arabian Gulf
is the pearl. You see the emblem of the pearl every-
where from the famous Pearl Roundabout of
Bahrain (now destroyed), to the pearl perched on top of the
tall column in Ittihad Square in Sharjah, to the water theme
park centred around hunting for a giant pearl in Abu Dhabi.
The pearl remains an enduring icon of the Arabian Gulf.

What I never appreciated was the sheer human cost of
bringing pearls into the market.

Until the 1930s, pearling was the major occupation of
the Gulf States. Every year young men and not-so-young
men would race out to the great pearling beds and spend
up to two months under the blazing sun, diving every ten
minutes or so, and spending on average up to three minutes under the water.

One of the earliest recorded descriptions of the pearl
diver was written by Ibn Battuta and is found in his book
Travels in Asia and Africa. He writes:

> Before diving, the diver puts on his face a sort of
> tortoise shell mask and a tortoise shell clip on his
> nose; then, he ties a rope around his waist and dives.
> They differ in their endurance under water... When he
> reaches the bottom of the sea, he finds the shells there
> stuck in the sand between small stones, and pulls them
> out by hand or cuts them loose with a knife which he
> has for that purpose, and puts them in a leather bag
> slung around his neck. When his breath becomes
> restricted, he pulls the rope and the man holding the
> rope on the boat feels the movement and pulls him
> up into the boat. The bag is taken from him and the
> shells are opened... The sultan takes his fifth and the
> remainder are bought by the merchants who are there
> in the boats. Most of them are creditors of the divers
> and they take the pearls in quittance of their debtor so
> much of it as is their due.[1]

Several hundred years later, another writer highlighted
the hardships of the divers:

> They used to dive down seventy metres or more on a
> single inhalation, aware that any delay in pulling them
> back up to the surface would result in brain damage
> or death. Many would return home suffering from
> exhaustion and malnutrition. Another peril facing the
> divers was infrequent yet deadly shark attacks.[2]

Along with dehydration and sunburn, they also faced
dangers from sea serpents and disease. All this was endured
for the hope of finding the pearl – the pearl of great value
which would release a man from his life of bondage and
buy his freedom from a harsh life of indentured labour.

Mohammed Al Suwaidi recalls his grandfather describing the life of a pearl diver:

He would ride out in 60-foot boats packed with dozens
of men and be out at sea for up to four months. Before
sunrise they would have two dates and drink a little water
and then dive for up to 14 hours, making as many as
250 descents in a day. Then in the evening they would
eat a meal on deck and drift off to sleep for a few hours
among thousands of stinking oyster shells, the flesh
rotting in the heat as they waited for them to open.[3]

These hardships are what made pearls so expensive.
Pearls were also the result of a rare and random event.
Khalaf Ahmad Al Habtoor, who grew up on the shores
of Dubai, estimated that only one in 10,000 wild oysters
would actually produce a natural pearl. Yet many families grew rich from pearling. John Steinbeck, a famous
American novelist, describes the formation and the rarity
of finding a pearl:

Light filtered down through the water to where the frilly
pearl oysters lay fastened to the rubbly bottom, a bottom
strewn with shells of broken, opened oysters... The grey
oysters with ruffles like skirts on the shells, the barnacle
encrusted oysters with little bits of weeds clinging to the
skirts and small crabs climbing over them. An accident
could happen to these oysters, a grain of sand could
lie in the folds of muscle and irritate the flesh until in
self-protection the flesh coated the grain with a layer of
smooth cement. But once started, the flesh continued to
coat the foreign body until it fell free in some tidal flurry
or until the oyster was destroyed... but the pearls were
accidents and the finding of one was luck, a little pat on
the back by God.[4]

With the advent of the Japanese cultured pearl, we forget
now how rare, how precious, and how random the success

of finding a great pearl was. But at the time of Jesus, they knew – and this was reflected in the great value of the pearl. The pearl was much coveted as a symbol of wealth and status. Thus, 'The famous Egyptian Princess Cleopatra was said to have a pearl necklace that was worth twenty five million denari (a denarius was one day's wages)'.[5]

Pliny, who described Roman history during and after the period in which Jesus lived, explained the importance of pearls in the region:

> Our ladies glory in having pearls suspended from their fingers, or two or three of them dangling from their ears, delighted even with the rattling of the pearls as they knock against each other... I once saw Lollia Paulina (died AD 48), the wife of Emperor Gaius... covered with emeralds and pearls, which shone in alternate layers upon her head, in her hair, in her wreaths, in her ears, upon her neck, in her bracelets, and on her fingers, and the value of which amounted to 40,000,000 sesterces; indeed she was prepared to prove the fact, by showing the receipts and acquittances.[6]

Pearls were, therefore, of great value. Their rarity, the hardships involved in extracting them from the sea, and their aesthetic beauty meant that the last thing you would do would be to cast them 'before swine, lest they trample them underfoot and turn to attack you' (Matthew 7:6). However, this quotation uses pearls as an allegory for the Gospel. As one of the most ancient scriptures says, 'The price of wisdom is above pearls' (Job 28:18).

This parable of Jesus about the pearl is, on the one hand, a very simple story to understand and yet on the other hand, profoundly and radically challenging. The implicit meaning is that if we only understood what Christ was speaking of, our response would be total commitment to the Kingdom of God. If we knew the true value of this pearl, then everything in our life would become subservient to the goal of ensuring that we realize this treasure.

What does Jesus really mean when he talks about the Kingdom of God? Again it is simple and yet profound. A kingdom refers to a domain under the rule of a King. Thus God's Kingdom is that domain or that area which is under the rule of God. But here's the thing: the Kingdom of God is not a geographically defined location, it is not a geopolitical reality that can be seen. Jesus said, 'My Kingdom is not of this world' (John 18:36). In other words, the Kingdom of God is a people who transcend nationality, nations, races, religion, and even time.

To become aware of this Kingdom is one thing, but to recognize its real value is quite another. It has become one of those phrases which has lost its meaning through over-familiarity and the passage of time. But for the original hearers of Jesus, people who were living desperate lives of hardship under Roman oppression, who were dreaming Messianic hopes and visions, ordinary men and women who were saying, 'There has got to be more to life than this!' Jesus' proclamation that the long awaited Kingdom of God had arrived and that the King was near – well, they would understand the value of that. It is worth noting that both in the Bible and the Qur'an the pearl is a symbol of eternal life and is used in scriptural imagery for describing heaven and paradise.[7]

We can summarize the teaching of Jesus on the pearl of great price as follows: The Kingdom of God is worth everything. Though hidden and rare, it represents the very essence of being in the presence of God. To be in possession of it, is to be in possession of eternity itself.

Do we really understand the value of pearls today? The pearling industry in its heyday could easily be referred to as a 'blood trade'. Men have suffered, gone into crippling debt, and some have died in order to make pearls available on the market. It is why they are so precious and valuable. Jesus intimated that the Kingdom of God is the same. A man sweated in pain and agony, and in the glare of the blazing sun he surrendered his life. It is his life that imbues the Kingdom of God with immeasurable value. This is the pearl of great value. To an Arab, growing up on the shores of the Arabian Gulf, fully acquainted with the human cost of pearling, this teaching attaches great value to a faith in something we cannot see.

1   Quoted in Khalaf Al Habtoor, *Khalaf Ahmad Al Habtoor: The Autobiography* (Dubai: Motivate Publishing, 2012), p. 47.

2   Ibid. p. 48.

3   Doran, J., Interview with Mohammed Al Suwaidi, *The National*, 7 June 2013, p. 4.

4   John Steinbeck, *The Pearl* (London: Puffin Books), p. 23.

5   David Wenham, *The Parables of Jesus* (Illinois: IVP, 1989) p. 208.

6   Hellyer, P. and Ziolkowski, M. *Emirates Heritage: Volume One. Proceedings of the 1ˢᵗ Annual Symposium on Recent Palaeontological & Archaeological Discoveries in the Emirates* (Al Ain: Zayed Centre for Heritage and History, 2005), p. 53.

7   In Revelations 21:21 we read that each of the twelve gates of the heavenly Jerusalem is made from a single pearl whereas in Sura 35:33 there is a description of those who have entered paradise as being adorned with gold and pearl bracelets.

FEET

WILL NEVER FORGET THE first time I saw a man shake the dust off his feet. He was a tourist who had been arrested by the police in a Gulf country for proselytizing Muslims. As he was escorted to the airport to be deported, he lifted his feet by the departures lounge and ceremoniously dusted them off. In doing so he was following instructions that Jesus left for his disciples:

> Whatever town or village you enter, search there for some worthy person and stay at their house until you leave. As you enter the home, give it your greeting. If the home is deserving, let your peace rest on it; if it is not, let your peace return to you. If anyone will not welcome you or listen to your words, leave that home or town and shake the dust off your feet.
>
> – Matthew 10:11–14

Feet are regarded as unclean in the Middle East. This is really not surprising as in a hot and humid climate, one's feet easily become sweaty, sticky, smelly, and, in a desert, very dusty and sandy. It is rude to point the soles of your feet at anyone in Arab company, and the greatest insult an Arab can do is to strike someone with their shoe.

Who could forget the scenes of the gigantic statue of Saddam Hussein being pulled down in Baghdad? As it crashed to the ground, Iraqi citizens instantly started slapping the statue with their sandals and shoes. It was a sign of utmost contempt. Or a few years later when another Iraqi citizen threw shoes at President George Bush as a sign of unrestrained rage.

This teaching of Jesus highlights a negative aspect of Middle Eastern culture. The positive aspect which Jesus refers to is the Arab code of hospitality. As his followers trekked around the region, he encouraged them to accept the hospitality of the local people. Instead of trying to push their own way into a new place, or have a preconceived strategy of who they would see and where they would go, Jesus encouraged them to go with the flow, to accept invitations from those who kept an open house and, through them, meet others.

He instructs them to greet the home with a salutation of peace, a tradition which is very much preserved among the Arab people today. 'As-salamu Alaikum!' is the oft-heard greeting in Arabic. It literally means 'Peace be upon you'.

There is something very profound happening when one declares peace on another. It is a statement of intent. In other words, the speaker is clearly indicating that they wish no harm on the other. In the Middle Eastern languages, 'Shalom' (Hebrew), 'Shlaam' (Aramaic) or 'Salaam' (Arabic) carry a concept much deeper than the English word 'Peace', which simply means the absence of conflict. In Arabic and Hebrew, the concept of peace includes the wish that the other person's life is whole and in complete alignment with the will and purpose of God. It is a prayer of benediction and good will. It tacitly acknowledges the essential need for God in the life of the other. Without God, there can be no wholeness, balance, or indeed, peace.

Jesus' instructions to his disciples takes place in the context of sending them out to be his representatives. The instructions that Jesus gave to his disciples should resonate with the culture today. He calls his followers to be peace-giving people who are to flow through Middle Eastern society through the hospitality of peace-loving hosts. The concept of peace has not been entirely forgotten in the West. While common greetings in Europe and America are conspicuously non-religious phrases like 'Hi! Hello! How are you!', the Western church still keeps alive the idea of sharing the peace and pronouncing a blessing on those gathered. In the Arabian Gulf however, the sharing of the peace is a multiple daily event, conveyed by the familiar greeting in Arabic *As-salamu Alaikum!*'

In a world marred by suspicion, conflict, and violence, the first step to bringing peace might be through pronouncing words of intent – 'Peace be upon you'.

WASHING FEET

There is a second incident in the Gospels, which concerns feet. It is a significant event as Jesus underlines his understanding of how religious people should function as leaders. In a society where people strove for status and there was a clear pecking order, servants were clearly at the bottom of the pile. One of the most menial jobs at that time was the washing of feet. As guests entered into a home, the servants would kneel before the newcomers and wash off the dirt and the grime from their feet with water. Feet, then as now, were regarded as the dirtiest part of the body. It is considered rude to point the soles of feet at another person, so to have to touch the feet, well, this was a job for the lowliest of servants.

... so he got up from the meal, took off his outer
clothing, and wrapped a towel around his waist. After
that, he poured water into a basin and began to wash
his disciple's feet, drying them with the towel that was
wrapped around him...'No,' said Peter, 'You shall never
wash my feet.'

Jesus answered, 'Unless I wash you, you have no part
with me.'

'Then, Lord,' Simon Peter replied, 'not just my feet but
my hands and my head as well!'

... When he had finished washing their feet, he put on
his clothes and returned to his place. 'Do you understand
what I have done for you?' he asked them. 'You call me
"Teacher"' and "Lord", and rightly so, for that is what I am.
Now that I, your Lord and Teacher, have washed your feet,
you also should wash one another's feet. I have set you
an example that you should do as I have done for you.
Very truly I tell you, no servant is greater than his master,
nor is a messenger greater than the one who sent him.
Now that you know these things, you will be blessed if
you do them.'

– John 13:4–17

It is difficult to communicate the shock of feet washing
outside the Middle East. Westerners wear shoes and socks,
even inside their homes, and when shoes and socks are
removed there is no immediate cause to wash their feet.
For Middle Easterners, the heat and humidity, the dust and
sand, and the normal use of sandals as footwear means
a completely different story. Sweaty, smelly feet are quite
simply not pleasant to be around! The job of washing feet
therefore goes to the lowliest of servants. The teaching of

Jesus then flies in the face of every ambitious religious leader and social climbing Middle Easterner. In effect, he said to his followers: 'If you want to be associated with me, you must humble yourself to the same level as the lowliest servant and serve others as better than yourselves'.

The tragedy of this teaching is that religious people worldwide have often failed to practically apply this instruction in their lives. Perhaps it is because they missed the cultural significance of what Jesus was doing. I suspect it is less to do with that and more to do with the common human desire to be ambitious and more powerful than others. Unfortunately, religious institutions such as the Church fall into the trap of naked pursuits of power and influence as much as anyone else.

I sometimes wonder what the contemporary application of this teaching might be in the Arabian Gulf. I cannot help but think of the ablutions, which take place daily in the GCC, not so much in residential homes, but in the mosques.

Muslims wash their feet (and their hands and face) in preparation for prayer, mainly as a way of coming before God in a 'clean' state, but I am sure that the person praying in the next line behind will be grateful for the foot hygiene of his fellow worshippers. While it is one thing for the worshipper to wash his own feet, is it possible that one application of Jesus' words in this context might be to exhort the worshippers to wash each other's feet as an expression of coming in humility before God in prayer? This indeed is a challenging thought and perhaps captures the impact and scandal of Jesus' leadership example in washing his disciples' feet.

All this underscores a core teaching, which Jesus consistently reinforced in his parables and lifestyle. He was convinced that the worship of the one God in heaven required humility; that is, humility in approaching God in prayer and humility in our relationships with other people.

He inferred that humility, which seeks to put the needs of our neighbours before our own is what defines a true worshipper of God. Of all the teachings of Jesus, this one is the easiest one to understand and the hardest to put into practice. The failure to live out this teaching has perhaps had the most severe consequences resulting in spiritual pride, witch-hunts, sectarianism, prejudices and violent persecution. The logical consequences of applying the teachings of Jesus in practice are truly hard to imagine, but the challenge is impossible for followers of Jesus to ignore. Jesus sums up this lesson later on in the same chapter with the following imperative:

> 'A new commandment I give you: Love one another. As I have loved you, so you must love one another. By this everyone will know that you are my disciples, if you love one another.'
>
> — John 13:34–35

PART THREE
WOMEN

OVERVIEW

THE THIRD ESSENTIAL COMPONENT of the Arab spirit, according to Allen, is the clearly prescribed role for women outlined in the religion of Islam and their place in tribal and family structures. It is always dangerous to generalize about gender roles in any region, let alone the Arabian Peninsula. However, while there may be striking cultural differences between the mountain village women of Oman and the nomadic tribal Bedouin women of Saudi Arabia, especially in their attire and lifestyle, the conservative expectations of tribe and family set widely recognized parameters for the roles of women across the region.

The teachers of the law and the Pharisees brought in a woman caught in adultery. They made her stand before the group and said to Jesus, 'Teacher, this woman was caught in the act of adultery. In the law Moses commanded us to stone such women. Now what do you say?' They were using this question as a trap, in order to have a basis for accusing him. But Jesus bent down and started to write on the ground with his finger. When they kept on questioning him, he straightened up and said to them, 'Let any one of you who is without sin be the first to throw a stone at her.' Again he stooped down and wrote on the ground. At this, those who heard began

to go away one at a time, the older ones first, until only
Jesus was left with the woman still standing there. Jesus
straightened up and asked her, 'Woman, where are they?
Has no one condemned you?'

'No one sir,' she said.

'Then neither do I condemn you,' Jesus declared. 'Go now
and leave your life of sin.'

— John 8:3–11

Nothing appears so curious to Westerners than seeing
groups of women clad head-to-toe in black, moving around
the shopping mall. Despite the sweltering heat, they are
draped in voluminous black *abayas*, their heads sheathed
in a black shawl known as a *hijab*, and for the more conservative women, their faces are completely veiled by a *niqab*
or a mask called a *burqa*. The effect is that their identity
remains a mystery and one is discouraged from engaging
with them in a public space. All this raises questions as
to what the life of a Gulf woman is really like.[1] Do they
resent the perceived restrictions placed upon them? How
does their seclusion from men impact their relationships
with men when they get married? Do they feel oppressed?

I remember in Kuwait, the distressed look on my
American Christian friend's face when the Kuwaiti Arab
man she was in conversation with talked about his two
wives. 'Poor women!' I heard her say as she shook her head
in reproof. The Orientalist tradition of the nineteenth century conjures up images of exotic women shuttered in their
Harems, forced into seclusion out of the sight of the rest
of the world, a picture swathed in oppression and sheer
boredom. A whole slew of contemporary books continue
to reinforce the view that the lot of a woman in Arabia is a
sorry one.[2]

Perhaps the number one question asked in any course on Islam or about the Middle East is, 'Why are women treated so badly?'

Laura Nader, an American-Arab anthropologist, exposes the underlying assumption behind this question, that 'Women in the West are far better off than women in the Middle East.'[3] The reporting of 'honour killings' and the alleged rapacity of Arab men is contrasted with the apparent freedom of Western women. Nader demonstrates this by referring to some surprising statistics, showing how a typical American woman faces a higher probability of being raped or murdered by her husband than an Arab woman does. Islam is somehow seen as the sole oppressor of women, yet the evidence shows that at the time of Jesus, women had equally tough times and faced varying degrees of exclusion and injustice.[4] The whole issue of veiling and covering up for example predates Islam and it has been suggested that the Arabian Peninsula woman's garb comes from pre-Islamic Jewish tribes.[5] This tradition of covering hair is not just an Islamic one. Today many conservative Christian Arab women cover their hair in worship, and in the Western Church, women (nuns) called by God to a spiritual vocation often cover their hair as an expression of obedience.

Jesus is often presented as a radical in terms of his treatment of women, even to the extent where he is seen as rejecting the teachings of the law as given by Moses. Hence, in the Gospel story (recorded at the beginning of this chapter) we see the religious experts attempting to trap Jesus, hauling before him a woman caught *in flagrante*. They wanted to see if Jesus would maintain his ethos of love and compassion and ignore the divine law, (which stipulates quite clearly that the penalty for women caught committing adultery is death by stoning) therefore publicly forcing Jesus to show disrespect to the revelation of God, or confirm the death penalty and show that his talk of love and compassion was just that – talk.

The woman is forced to stand in front of the group of men. Having been caught in the act, it is safe to say that she is not dressed for the occasion. Her shame is complete. The religious leaders then begin haranguing Jesus for his answer as to what they should do with her. Jesus' response is to bend over and start writing in the sand. What he wrote in the sand, we can only speculate. One of the most intriguing suggestions is recorded by William Barclay:

> The Armenian commentary and text translates the passage this way: 'He himself bowing his head, was writing with his finger on the earth to declare their sins; and they were seeing their several sins written on the stones.'
> The suggestion is that Jesus was writing in the dust the sins of the very men who were accusing the woman. There may be something in that. The normal Greek word for 'to write' is *graphein*; but here the word used is *katagraphein*, which can mean to write down a record against someone. It may be that Jesus was confronting those self-confident sadists with the record of their own sins.[6]

This may explain why the accusers of the woman drifted away one by one leaving only the stunned victim herself still standing before Jesus. She is dismissed with the instruction to leave her life of shame and begin afresh. As Michele Guinness commented:

> Jesus did not alter or override Old Testament theology. He interpreted it, enhanced it, divested it of the cultural flotsam and jetsam attached to it by the tide of time and human hypocrisy, and tempered it with mercy. This liberating, life-changing approach is particularly evident when he does not condemn the adulterous woman,

but challenges her male accusers (who are indifferent
to the fact that her male partner in crime has done a
vanishing act) to cast the first stone if they dare.[7]

Given that the penalty for adultery today in parts of the
Islamic world is, at worst, death by stoning or at best, a
flogging, this story still holds relevance for some Muslim
women who face a similar predicament.

It must be stressed that Jesus did not take the crime of
adultery lightly. Rather, he gave her a second chance and
warned her not to repeat her behaviour. His ire though is
really reserved for the religious leaders. Their plotting and
attitude had reduced the woman to a tool. They humiliated
and dehumanized her, and in their cruelty there was no
compassion or respect. One author even speculated that the
male adulterer had been paid by them to set the woman up
so they could bring her as a case to test Jesus. Jesus saw her
as an individual. He saw the frightened and broken woman
in contrast to the self-righteous arrogance of a murderous
and cynical religious group. He turned the tables on them.
Somehow through his doodling in the sand, Jesus exposed
their hypocrisy, forcing them to slink away in shame.

In this section of Jesus' teachings, we look at how he
treated women and what he taught them during his time
in Palestine.

---

1   For a sympathetic description of life as a Gulf woman read Patricia Holton's
    Mother Without a Mask.
2   Jean Sasson has been a prolific author in this regard and has written several exposés of
    life for royal women in Saudi Arabia. Her first bestseller *Princess* (2001) inspired a new
    genre of post-orientalist writing.
3   Nader, L., *Culture and Dignity: Dialogues between the Middle East and the West*
    (London: Wiley & Blackwell, 2013), p. 12.
4   Leonard Swidler, *Women in Judaism* (New York: Scarecrow Press, 1976).
5   G. D. Newby, *A History of the Jews of Arabia* (USA: Columbia, 1988).
6   William Barclay, *The Gospel of John: Volume 2* (The Daily Bible Study Series,
    Edinburgh: The Saint Andrew Press, 1975), p. 3.
7   Michele Guinness, *Woman: The Full Story* (Michigan: Zondervan, 2003), p. 107.

SCENT

I N EVERY SHOPPING MALL in the Gulf you will find at least
one shop dedicated to the selling of perfumes and incense called *Oud*. Often, the shop will advertise its
presence by burning the *Oud*, thus ambushing their customers with the powerful scent wafting around the souk.

When visiting a Majlis or a home, a common tradition is
that the host brings around a container from which clouds
of incense pour forth. The guests waft the incense onto
their clothes and their hair. Sometimes the incense burner
is placed on the carpet and the guests in their robes step
over it so that the smoke rises up between their legs and
out through their necklines. In a sweaty and humid climate, it is one way of keeping unwanted aromas at bay.

Powerful perfumes are popular in the Arabian Gulf.
Walking down the street in Kuwait, Dubai, or Abu Dhabi,
one's sense of smell is constantly overcome by the scents
worn by both Arab men and women. It is a big industry
and one that generates wealth. Perfumes are expensive and
can indicate wealth in the same way a car can.

It was the same in the days of Jesus. Perfumes and
spices were essential for disguising bodily odours. They
were also used for embalming. In the heat, dead bodies
decay very quickly and perfumes disguised the smell of a

putrid corpse. Finally, incense, especially frankincense, was used in worship as a symbol of prayer. The smoke of the Frankincense rising to the heavens became a potent sign of the hopes and petitions of the people to God, as if to say 'May my prayer be set before you like incense' (Psalm 141:2). In John's Gospel we read of the following incident:

> Then Mary took about half a litre of pure nard, an expensive perfume; she poured it on Jesus' feet and wiped his feet with her hair. And the house was filled with the fragrance of the perfume.
>
> – John 12:3

By any reckoning this was a lavish act. There was an instant protest from one of the disciples of Jesus who recognized the monetary value of the perfume. One year's wages had just been poured out over Jesus' feet. In response, Jesus said, 'It was intended that she should save this perfume for the day of my burial' (John 12:7).

The perfume was a sign of worship. Mary held nothing back from Jesus – it was her gift to him. Jesus reminds the witnesses of this anointing by Mary about the other main use of perfume and spice – that of preparing a dead body for burial. He indicates in this incident that already he knew his fate. He was moving towards his destiny of crucifixion and he was signalling that this was his intent and purpose. It was no mistake that he died. Jesus interpreted his life through the prophecies found in the Old Testament. Those prophecies spoke of one who would become a suffering servant who would be put to death.

However, there is so much more to this story than a woman anointing Jesus' feet with perfume. On another level, Jesus was also making a statement about women. Traditionally the woman who poured perfume over his feet is identified as Mary Magdalene who has been portrayed as a loose woman or prostitute (though the Bible does not actually refer to her as a prostitute). The Gospel describes her as a woman who had been set free from demon possession.[1] Like the Samaritan woman at the well, Mary would have been an object of scorn and derision from her community and perhaps regarded with some fear. Religious leaders would have avoided the company of such a woman due to fear of pollution (from her alleged immoral sexuality and demonic influences), and certainly would have been repulsed by her touching them. Jesus shocked his company by allowing her to anoint his feet and accepting her presence. Luke described the scene vividly:

> A woman in that town who lived a sinful life learned that Jesus was eating at the Pharisee's house, so she came there with an alabaster jar of perfume. As she stood behind him at his feet weeping, she began to wet his feet with her tears. Then she wiped them with her hair, kissed them and poured perfume on them. When the Pharisee who had invited him saw this, he said to himself, 'If this man were a prophet, he would know who is touching him and what kind of woman she is – that she is a sinner.'
>
> – Luke 7:37–39

Pharisees were extremely devout men. They lived by religious laws and sought to please God by submitting to an interpretation of these laws and their niceties written down by scholars. The central purpose of the law is to enable a worshiper to maintain ritual purity in the presence of God. To be touched by a woman who was a 'sinner' would defile the body of a worshipper. Jesus would know that this would be a concern of his host, and the presence of Mary in his home would have been a source of discomfort. However, it seems that the Pharisee was prepared to undergo this discomfort in order to see how Jesus would respond to the woman. A truly righteous person, in the mind of the Pharisee, would have sent Mary fleeing from the house, and a man claiming to be a prophet would have no end of religious indignation reserved for such a 'sinner'. That Jesus did not do this raised a suspicion in the mind of Simon the Pharisee who questioned both Jesus' status as a prophet and his righteousness.

What happened next suggests that Jesus knew what the Pharisee was thinking and indeed was anticipating his response. Luke then records Jesus' response:

> Simon, I have something to tell you... two people owed
> money to a certain money-lender. One owed him five
> hundred denari and the other fifty. Neither of them had
> the money to pay him back, so he forgave the debts of
> both. Now which of them will love him more?
>
> – Luke 7:40–42

The answer is obvious, and Simon the Pharisee gave the correct response that the one who owed more would be more grateful.

Then Jesus gestured towards the woman and went on to teach a lesson that stunned his Middle Eastern audience:

> Do you see this woman? I came into your house. You
> did not give me any water for my feet, but she wet my
> feet with her tears and wiped them with her hair. You
> did not give me a kiss, but this woman, from the time
> I entered, has not stopped kissing my feet. You did not

put oil on my head, but she has poured perfume on
my feet. Therefore, I tell you, her many sins have been
forgiven – for she loved much. But he ho has been
forgiven little loves little.

Then Jesus said to her, 'Your sins are forgiven.'

– Luke 7:44–48

Jesus challenged the conventional religious wisdom of
Middle Eastern culture, namely that one strives to please
God by following religious ritual and law. The more one
keeps themselves from sinning and remains ritually pure,
the more virtuous and righteous they are perceived to be,
both by their peers and themselves. While the desire to
please God is obviously one Jesus affirmed, he attacked
the spiritual pride and the toxic lack of humanity that the
pursuit of holiness had produced in his fellow country-
men. Instead of measuring their status against the grace
and mercy of God, they competed with members of their
own community to see who was most fastidious in keeping the law. In the end, they lost sight of God and their
own need to be thankful resulting in an arrogance that
demeaned others.

The teaching of Jesus emphasized the grace and mercy
of God, who reaches out to the sinner and that the only true
response of the worshipper is gratitude and an amazed
relief that a Holy God had condescended to draw them into
His presence. In other words, Mary the sinner was more in
a state of God's grace than the pious Pharisee, for she knew
the true worth of the debt she owed.

The final sting in the tale was Jesus' announcement
to the woman that her sins were now forgiven. In a religious system where forgiveness was 'bought' from God

through expensive blood sacrifices made in the temple by a qualified priest, Jesus' words hinted at a very different mode for the sinner. His words would have been regarded as blasphemous, for the Pharisees believed that only God ultimately had the power to forgive. In offering a statement of forgiveness to Mary, Jesus was doing something unthinkable. He was assuming the right to do something which belonged to God and God alone. 'The other guests began to say among themselves, "who is this who even forgives sins?"' (Luke 7:49).

This is the unanswered question which Jesus leaves hanging in the air.

For Mary, Jesus was the man who healed her from demon possession. He was the religious leader who showed her compassion and did not reject her or despise her, like other men did. Jesus was the man she followed out of gratitude and worship.

Her actions in pouring scent on the feet of Jesus proved to be prophetic, for the next instance in which perfume is mentioned in the Gospel relates to his death.

THE FINAL ANOINTING OF JESUS

After Jesus died, his body was taken down from the cross and the women came to prepare his body for burial. We read that Nicodemus[2] provided a mixture of aloes and myrrh, about seventy five pounds. 'Taking Jesus' body, they wrapped it with the spices in strips of linen' (John 19:39–40).

The striking thing about this passage is the sheer quantity of spices used to embalm Jesus' body. It was excessive. But again, the spices reveal a story of worship and it signalled from Nicodemus a powerful expression of his conviction that Jesus was a Messianic King. According to the Jewish Midrash, only royalty had the privilege to be buried with such excessive amounts of spices and perfumes. It was a coded message. The sheer excess and amount of spices used to embalm the body sent a declaration. It was a declaration of faith to those who followed Jesus as King.

---

1   Luke 8:1 'Mary called Magdalene from whom seven demons came out.'
2   Nicodemus was a powerful religious teacher who was intrigued by the teachings and person of Jesus. We first encounter him in John 3.

WATER

Jacob's well was there, and Jesus, tired as he was from the journey, sat down by the well. It was about noon. When a Samaritan woman came to draw water, Jesus said to her, 'Will you give me a drink?' (His disciples had gone into the town to buy food.) The Samaritan woman said to him, 'You are a Jew and I am a Samaritan woman. How can you ask me for a drink?' (For Jews do not associate with Samaritans).

Jesus answered her, 'If you knew the gift of God and who it is that asks you for a drink, you would have asked him and he would have given you living water.'

'Sir,' the woman said, 'you have nothing to draw with and the well is deep. Where can you get this living water? Are you greater than our father Jacob, who gave us the well and drank from it himself, as did also his sons and his livestock?'

Jesus answered, 'Everyone who drinks this water will be thirsty again, but whoever drinks the water I give them will never thirst. Indeed, the water I give them will become in them a spring of water welling up to eternal life.'

– John 4:6–14

THE ISLAND OF ABU DHABI is in fact named after a well. The story goes that hunters on the mainland tracked a gazelle (known in Arabic as *'dhabi'*) to the shore, and then in the morning realized that the gazelle had forded the waters over to the island across from them. The hunting party crossed over to the island and discovered the drinking hole that the gazelle were headed for. The island, or rather the well, was subsequently named Abu Dhabi, or in English, 'Father of the Gazelle', which was a colloquial way of attributing the water in the well as a source of life.[1]

One of the intriguing geographical features of Bahrain is that there are underground freshwater springs that flow under the Gulf and supply the island with potable water. Edmund O'Sullivan describes how this came to be:

> The rise and fall of the sea made Bahrain. At the peak of the last Great Ice Age, most of North America, Europe and Northern Asia lay buried beneath a thick glacial layer and the Gulf was mainly dry land... It was divided by the lazy meanderings of a river running from the Shatt al-Arab to the ocean lapping the Strait of Hormuz... But water trapped within the aquifers was forced to the surface to make the island an oasis.[2]

Hence the name Bahrain, which literally means 'two seas' (one saltwater and one freshwater).

In Oman and the UAE, the visitor can only but marvel at the skill with which local people created *falajs*, manmade water canals both above and below ground in order to water gardens and oases sometimes high in the mountains.

Meanwhile, over in Kuwait a famous water source can be found on the island of Failaka which was home to an ancient cult.

It centres on the life of the Green Man (*Al Khidr*)
who is said to have been the only soul to have gained
immortality by tasting the water of life (*Ma'ul Hayat*).
Al Khidr lived on Failaka and transformed it into a
green and pleasant land by sinking deep-water wells.
According to tradition, Khidr became a companion
of Alexander and Jesus.[3]

Clearly, in an arid desert climate, water is essential. The
English explorer, Sir Wilfred Thesiger, in his travels across
the Empty Quarter (a vast sandy desert which stretches
across the Arabian peninsula), described how his Bedouin
company approached water wells with great caution and,
while using a well, were on alert for hostile enemies who
would object to their water supplies being used.[4]

H. B. Tristam begins his book *Eastern Customs in Arab
Lands* with this personal experience. He was sitting
beside a well when an Arab woman came down from the
hills above to draw water. She unfolded and opened her
goatskin bottle, and then untwined a cord, and attached
it to a small leather bucket which she carried, by means
of which she slowly filled her goatskin, fastened its
mouth, placed it on her shoulder, and bucket in hand,
climbed the mountain. Shortly after that an Arab man
came toiling up the steep footpath. Heated and wearied
from his journey, he turned aside to the well, knelt and
peered wistfully down, but he had nothing to draw the
water with and the well was deep. He lapped a little
moisture from the water spilled by the woman earlier
and, disappointed, passed on.[5]

Water was a scarce and precious resource. The nomads
of Arabia shaped their seasonal travels around the pursuit

of access to water. It is not surprising then that water itself became an allegory for spiritual truth that gives life. It is fascinating then, but perhaps not that surprising, that there is a Gulf version of water being the source of immortality or eternal life.

Jesus' encounter with the Samaritan woman is an enlightening account on several levels. Firstly, we learn how Jesus ignored the norms of local culture in order to teach not just the woman but also his own disciples spiritual lessons transcending culture, time, and space. Secondly, we learn how he encountered the 'other', that is someone from a different faith and race. Finally, there was his bold claim that she was in the presence of someone who would give her spiritual truth, which would be like water, satisfying her thirst for truth and meaning. All this dialogue took place over a famous water well with historical connotations.

The role of women in Jesus' day was clearly prescribed by culture and religion. There was segregation between the sexes, and one of the reasons for this was men fearing pollution by women. One of the things that made a person ritually unclean for worship was contact with blood, so to accidentally come into contact with a menstruating woman was to make a man (or another woman) unclean. The concept of pollution and the impact that this would have on being prepared for worship is a feature found throughout societies in the Middle East and the Arabian Gulf.

Andrew Rippin observes what traditional interpretations of the role of women means in Islam today:

> In practice, women have been excluded from substantial areas of Islamic ritual. Menstruation, while not implying a ritual contagion in Islam, serves as a barrier to ritual performance for the woman concerned. Thus while men

have nothing to fear from women being present at prayer,
the ritual status of a woman would be on full public view
as she could only come when she was ritually pure.[6]

Some cultures in the Arabian Peninsula view women
as threatening in terms of their sexuality. Men took on the
responsibility of guarding the honour (chastity) of women,
and the failure to deliver her on her first wedding night
as a virgin brought great shame on the family and the
woman. The prescribed legal penalty for such shame was
death. Another response to such shame was to seclude
the offending woman from society. In its extreme form,
this meant the woman literally being forcibly confined to
a cell or room in the family home, and in its mildest form
being shunned by family and community members. The
latter makes for a lonely and pitiable existence. Going
out to do chores meant running a gauntlet of jibes and
prejudice from family and neighbours. It was better to
be alone.

The Samaritan woman at the well was one such woman.
Normally, collecting water from the well was a group activity for women. They would collect the water first thing in
the cool of the morning, and the heavy task was lightened
by going as a social group. There was of course an added
benefit in that the group provided a layer of protection
from any unwanted attention. The fact that the Samaritan
woman was coming alone to the well in the midday heat
speaks volumes about her treatment by members of her
own community. She was a woman marked by shame.
The proper response then from any person of religion or
faith would therefore be to shun her. She would be seen as
a threat because of her perceived out-of-control sexuality
and as such would be seen as an agent of pollution. That
she is still alive would have been seen as an act of mercy;

the community were legally entitled to stone her to death. The honour of women is still a live concern of families in the Middle East. Media coverage of so-called 'honour killings' only serve to illustrate the strong sense of shame linked to sexually deviant behaviour.

To avoid any such possible 'wrong' encounters, the public behaviour of women was carefully regulated. It was therefore unusual for a woman to be alone with a man who was not related to her. This could be interpreted in a most undesirable way with dire consequences for the woman.

This explains the surprise of Jesus' disciples when they saw him conversing with a woman who was on her own. But their surprise had an extra layer of prejudice. Not only was Jesus talking to a woman on her own, thereby risking the chance of ceremonial and spiritual pollution along with his personal reputation, but she was also a Samaritan. She was a member of group who were traditionally reviled and despised as 'heretics' by the Jews. For a Jew, even to be seen in the company of a Samaritan was equal to collaborating with the enemy.

THE SAMARITANS

No one is really sure of the origins of the Jewish/Samaritan split. The little we know about the Samaritans at the time of Jesus is that they had a temple on Mount Gerizim, which was near the ancient village of Shechem. The Old Testament celebrates Shechem as the place where Abram renewed his covenant with God and built an altar.[7] Here in the same place, Jacob (Abram's grandson) pitched his tent, bought land, and raised an altar to the God of Israel.[8] The bones of Joseph were buried at Shechem by his family. Thus Shechem was an esteemed centre of worship, and the locals celebrated their home as a place where the Lord met with His people. It was near this place that Joshua, when leading the invasion of the Hebrews into the land of Canaan, had his army renew their pledge to God:

> On that day Joshua made a covenant for the people, and there at Shechem he drew up for them decrees and laws. And Joshua recorded these things in the Book of the Law of God. Then he took a large stone and set it up there under the oak tree near the holy place of the Lord. 'See!' he said to all the people. 'This stone will be a witness against us. It has heard all the words that the Lord has said to us. It will be a witness against you if you are untrue to your God.'
>
> – Joshua 24:25–27

So when Solomon erected a temple at Jerusalem and declared it the centre of worship for all Israel, the people of Shechem (based in Samaria) were understandably aggrieved. Their refusal to acknowledge Jerusalem as a place of worship led to the bitter division between Samaritan and Jew, which continues to this day.

Yet the Samaritans had much in common with the Jewish faith at the time of Jesus. They had a system of sacrifice, they faithfully read the Pentateuch (the first five books of the Old Testament), and they devoted themselves to following religious laws. Essentially, the Samaritans shared the same history as the Jews and the same faith. As is often the case, the worst feuds are those that take place in the same family. The acrimony of this feud is reflected in the instructions of the Jewish rabbis to their people, advising them that, 'The daughters of Samaritans menstruate from birth (thus permanently polluted) and anything they touch is therefore unclean.'[9]

The Jews at the time of Jesus would often avoid the risk of meeting 'polluted' Samaritans by taking a lengthy circuitous route around Samaria. Jesus, in contrast, walked straight through the middle of Samaritan territory, and in his parable highlighting who was the best neighbour, used a Samaritan as the hero of the story, all of which was very provocative to the Jewish audience listening to him.

Jesus thus violated multiple rules of his local culture. He talked with a woman on her own. Even worse than that, he spoke to a woman of dubious reputation (Jesus certainly knew of her reputation and revealed to her his knowledge of her history of multiple relationships with men). Finally, he spoke to a member of a heretical and polluted community.

What did he do that was so radical? He entered into dialogue with her. He asked for a drink of water. He recognized her as an individual and had a conversation that led to a spiritual truth being proclaimed. There was no approbation, disapproval, or prejudice.

So what did he say? Unsurprisingly, given the context of where they were meeting, he talked about water. After exclaiming her shock of being asked by a man for a drink, and a Jewish one at that, Jesus responded by provoking her curiosity with regards to his identity ('If you knew who was asking you for a drink you would ask him for living water'). The phrase 'living water' was a colloquialism for running water. Fresh running water would be far more refreshing than the brackish stagnant water of the well. The woman immediately leaps to the defense of the well and her ancestor who allegedly discovered it. Jacob, the famed father of the even more famed Joseph (he of the technicolour coat), was revered by the Samaritans as their great patriarch and leader, and cherished amongst his legacy was the well. 'Are you implying that you could have found a better water source than the great patriarch?' is the meaning of the woman's tart response to Jesus' pitch.

Jesus then continues to provoke the woman's interest by highlighting that the woman's thirst would be satisfied by this living water and she need never be thirsty again. Again, the woman is interpreting Jesus' comment literally, and she asks him to reveal the source of this living water.

Finally, Jesus shocks the woman more by revealing his knowledge of her status in her community as a woman who has been rejected because of the stigma of her broken relationships. The slow realization that the stranger talking to her had a prophetic gift stirs her mind and emotions towards deeper issues. The conversation now turns to spiritual truth. The woman, in default mode as a Samaritan, asserts that the best place to worship surely would be the mountain where her temple was based.

It is at this point in this conversation when Jesus imparts his teaching on the nature of God and worship. He said:

> A time is coming when you will worship the Father neither on this mountain nor in Jerusalem. You Samaritans worship what you do not know; we worship what we know, for salvation is from the Jews. Yet a time is coming and has now come when the true worshippers will worship the Father in the Spirit and in truth, for they are the kind of worshippers the Father seeks. God is spirit, and his worshippers must worship in the Spirit and in truth.
>
> – John 4:21–24

Jesus is highlighting a vital truth. There is a human tendency to imagine God as residing only in certain places and environments. Thus the Jews were convinced that the only way to have a true encounter with God was in the 'holy' temple in Jerusalem. The Samaritans imitated this conviction except they insisted God could only truly be encountered on their mountain. Jesus is effectively saying that what really counts is the attitude of the worshipper, not the location. While there are some places, which are venerated because they have the history of a divine encounter, in reality we can worship God anywhere.

In the Middle East I am often sharply reminded of this teaching when driving along remote roads. I often come across cars parked at the side of the road and a little further away from the car, prostrated on a rug, is a Muslim performing his prayers – in the middle of nowhere. For these Muslims, there is no need for a temple or a magnificent mosque. They faithfully pray in the wilderness and unknowingly live out the teachings of Jesus – we can encounter God anywhere as long as our hearts are turned in prayer and worship God through the presence of his Holy Spirit.

The outcome of the meeting with the woman at the well concludes with the woman recognizing Jesus as the Christ, and she returns to her village to challenge her community to come and encounter Jesus. The village, in curiosity and excitement, turn out to encounter Jesus for themselves.

One little known observation on this story is that it is the record of the very first Christian missionary and evangelist, and this exalted role in history belongs to a woman.

When we look at the structure of Jesus' dialogue we again see a poet's technique and rhetorical style emerge. William Barclay highlights what happens:

> Jesus' technique is that he first makes a statement,
> which is taken in the wrong sense by the person it
> is directed at. Jesus then remakes the statement in
> an even more vivid way. It is still misunderstood;
> and then Jesus compels the person with whom he
> is speaking to discover and face the truth for herself
> or himself. That was his usual way of teaching;[10] and
> it was a most effective way, for, as someone has said
> 'There are certain truths which a man cannot accept;
> he must discover them for himself.'[11]

Water is precious, especially in a desert environment, and living water running and flowing continuously is even more precious and coveted. The teaching of Jesus imparted to the woman at the well suggests that she, in her shame and need, was not dependent on following the prescribed traditions of her culture but that she could be liberated by encountering God at any time and in any place – just as her ancestor Jacob did. More pointedly and controversially, Jesus offers himself as a source of that living water, and that through him would be the means to worship God in spirit and truth. The implications of Jesus' words seem to be that, at any time, in any place, a real encounter with the God who created the heavens and the earth can be found in Jesus.

---

1   Christopher Davidson, *Abu Dhabi: Oil and Beyond* (London: Hurst & Company 2009), p. 6.

2   Edmund O'Sullivan, *The New Gulf: How Modern Arabia is Changing the World for Good* (Dubai: Motivate Publishing, 2008), pp. 186 –187.

3   Ibid. pp. 172–173.

4   Wilfred Thesiger, *Arabian Sands* (London: Longmans, 1959).

5   William Barclay, *The Gospel of John: Volume 1* (The Daily Bible Study Series, Edinburgh: The Saint Andrew Press, 1975), p. 153.

6   Andrew Rippin, *Muslims: Their Religious Beliefs and Practices, Volume 2: The Contemporary Period* (London: Routledge, 1993), p. 117.

7   Genesis 12:6

8   Genesis 33:18–19

9   Green, J. B., McKnight, S. and Marshall, H. (Eds), *Dictionary of Jesus and the Gospels: A Compendium of Contemporary Biblical Scholarship* (Leicester: IVP, 1992), p. 728.

10   Another classic example of this can be found in Jesus' conversation with Nicodemus in John 3.

11   Barclay, Vol. 1, p. 152.

HOSPITALITY

As Jesus and his disciples were on their way, he came to a village where a woman named Martha opened her home to him. She had a sister called Mary, who sat at the Lord's feet listening to what he said. But Martha was distracted by all the preparations that had to be made. She came to him and asked, 'Lord, don't you care that my sister has left me to do all the work by myself? Tell her to help me!'

'Martha, Martha,' the Lord answered, 'you are worried and upset about many things, but only one thing is needed. Mary has chosen what is better and it will not be taken away from her.'

– Luke 10:38–42

As I write this, it is Ramadan. Every day Muslim women work incredibly hard in the kitchen to feed family and friends in preparation for when the fast is broken. It is a matter of pride that good quality food is served in abundance. For the last two weeks now I have attended Ramadan meals and the tables have heaved with food. While it seems wasteful to Westerners, to the Arab it is a measure of their generous desire to make sure that their guests want for nothing. It is, in fact, nothing less than a religious duty, and the family's honour and pride are reflected in their hospitality. Gina Crocetti Benesh, in her book describing the culture of the United Arab Emirates, explains why hospitality is so important in the Arabian peninsula:

> Hospitality may be the single most important law of the desert. Without it, people travelling in the desert away from their groups would die. Even poor people are required to feed and shelter strangers and guests for an obligatory three days. The guest may leave after a few days without ever stating his name or business because it is rude for the host to ask.[1]

This seems to have been the case for a very long time in the Middle East. Remember the story of Abraham, mentioned at the beginning of this book, and his hospitality to the three men?[2] Sarah, his wife, worked flat out to make sure that the guests had a sumptuous meal, which would honour her guests and Abraham himself.

So we need to understand that when Jesus arrived at Martha's home, Martha was compelled by her Middle Eastern culture and tradition to provide the very best hospitality. I remember reading this and being puzzled about what the big deal was for Martha. 'Come on Martha, give Jesus a cup of tea and join Mary!' That was my very English way of interpreting this story. I had overlooked two things. First of all, hospitality for Martha was not about offering a cup of tea but a full blown meal, which in the absence of a Carrefour Hypermarket or Lulu supermarket (popular shops found throughout the Gulf), meant serious, time-consuming food preparation. Secondly, Jesus was not alone, Jesus was travelling around the countryside with an entourage of at least seventy people. Having all these people show up to your villa would be a challenge for the most seasoned cook. No wonder Martha was stressed and annoyed with Mary for not helping.

The surprising thing is that Mary did not help. She certainly would have been aware of the work involved and of the implication to family honour if hospitality failed. Yet she continued to ignore what surely must have been a less-than-subtle signal from Martha and other family members by listening to Jesus.

To a Middle Easterner, the issue was straightforward. Martha was in the right and Mary was in the wrong. Mary's duty, according to religious and cultural tradition, was to ensure her family provided hospitality to their honoured guests. Middle Eastern women would have shaken their heads and scolded Mary for her shame and laziness, and Middle Eastern men would have been shocked at her lack of regard for the family name.

So when Martha demanded that Jesus challenge Mary's lack of action, his response was completely contrary to what everyone else thought. In the end, it was Martha who was chided. The culture of hospitality was set aside while Jesus taught a lesson which has resonated through the ages.

Martha was a conscientious and hard worker. Her activism and busyness would have received approval from all who knew her. Yet Jesus challenged the conventional view that being busy alone is a virtue. He pointed out that Martha was indeed busy and distracted by many things and these caused her a great deal of stress. Stress, he pointed out, that took her away from things that really count in life. He then commended Mary for the very thing that everyone else condemned her for. She took time out to listen to Jesus. The clear implication being then, at that point in time, that listening to Jesus was a higher duty than hospitality.

Why did Jesus allow Mary to neglect her duty? Was it because Jesus was on the way to Jerusalem where he knew he was going to face punishment and death? The knowledge that his time was running out would certainly make him appreciate the time he had left with those who did choose to listen to him. Maybe it was possible that Mary was somehow intuitive to this, and that caused her to ignore other pressing demands and simply focus on being sat at the feet of Jesus for a while. Whatever the reason, Jesus said that the choice Mary made would have lasting consequences. She had chosen the better thing and taken time out to listen to Jesus.

All this would have been, and still would be, a radical departure from what is seen as the sacred duty of hospitality. For the Gulf Arab and expatriates who live in the Gulf, there is an implicit challenge in Jesus' response to Martha. Namely, it forces us to re-evaluate the importance of our activities and whether or not the things we do count in the perspective of eternity.

The pursuit of a successful career and wealth is an activity which dominates modern day Arabia and one in which huge amounts of energy is consumed. In the midst of the clamour of the workplace and the market, the Middle Easterner also has the demands of the traditional culture of hospitality and commitment to family and guests. How does one escape the pressure of such demands? Demands which, when broken down and examined in the cold light of day, are usually exposed as shallow and temporal. Jesus' challenge to Martha and others who are prone to a culture of the 'urgent' is to stop and make time to take in teaching which will stay with us and shape our characters and eternal destiny.

One thing I have come to appreciate about living in the Arabian Gulf is the month of Ramadan. It is amazing to see how complete societies slow down and daytime activities grind to a halt to allow time to pray and fast. There are of course those who ignore the religious aspect of Ramadan, and for them the opportunity to heed Jesus' teachings passes by. This is especially challenging for Arab women given the expectation to entertain guests on an almost daily basis. Does the story of Martha and Mary continue to resonate with Gulf Arab women today?

---

1   Benesh, p. 76.
2   Genesis 18:1–8

PART FOUR
LANGUAGE

OVERVIEW

T HE LAST ESSENTIAL COMPONENT of the Arab spirit as defined by Mark Allen is the definitive role of language. Every culture is united largely by language and so there is nothing unusual or distinctive about that, but the Gulf Arabs have elevated the role of language to a new level because Arabic is widely regarded as the vehicle of God's speech. It is not the language of mortal humans but the language of deity. The divine revelation of the Holy Qur'an provides the lectionary which peppers the daily dialogue of the Gulf Arab and the ability to compose and recite poetry is seen as the epitome of learning in the Gulf region.

The people of the Middle East have a longstanding oral tradition and Jesus was part of this. He knew the power of stories and poetry, and it comes as no surprise that he employed the rhetorical skills familiar to the Semitic people to great effect. In this section, I will highlight how the teachings of Jesus were presented in a highly skilful manner, employing poetical structures which would enable his message to be 'sticky'[1] and thus remembered and passed on.

The Gulf Arabs also treasure poetry and storytelling. I have been in several meetings where a poet was invited to recite his (and on one occasion, her) latest creation. The appreciative responses to their words exceeded anything one witnesses in the West. What is clear is that Arabs, while they understand the abstract structures of poetry, primarily enjoy words as an acoustical aesthetic. They *experience* poetry as a regular feature of their lives.

Arabic has a long and celebrated oral tradition and among the most revered members of the Arabic speaking community are the poets. Jesus himself spoke Aramaic which is a sister language to Arabic and thus intelligible to the Arabic speaker. So it is no surprise then to find that the poetical devices used in the rich oral tradition of Aramaic culture are reflected in the Arabic language.

A distinctive feature of Middle Eastern society and the Gulf is the oral tradition of the people. This produces a deep respect for the poets and the storytellers who are highly esteemed because they are seen as the custodians of tradition. Poetry is regarded as a powerful tool for passing on teachings and history. Some of the suras of the Holy Qur'an are written in a style of Arabic poetry, which enables easier memorization and ensures that it will be passed on without alteration.

Songs and poetry in the Arabic tradition also serve more pragmatic purposes. There are some songs of the pearl divers, the length and metre of which coincide with the amount of time the average pearl diver can hold his breath under water. Longitude and latitude in navigation in the desert were calculated by estimating the distance between the horizon and the stars and by traditional 'pacing' songs which allowed the travellers to estimate distance.

Neal Robinson, who has a deep appreciation for the genius of Arabic poetry, especially in the Holy Qur'an, explains how much is lost when we translate Arabic into English. As an example, he translates the verses in which the Prophet Muhammad (PBUH) is commanded by God:

Read in the name of thy Lord who created.
He created man from a blood clot.
Read; and thy Lord is the most generous,
He who has taught with the pen
Taught man what he did not know.

– Sura 96:1–5

The above verses also happen to be the very first words of the Qur'an, chronologically speaking. Much is lost in the English rendering, but in the Arabic transliteration we see the power of the poetry in the Qur'an emerging:

Iqra' bismi rabbi-ka 'l-ladhi khalaq
Khalaqa 'l-insana min 'alaq
Iqra' wa-rabbu-ka 'l-akram
Al-ladhi 'allama bi-'l-qalam
'allama 'l-insana ma lam ya'lam

Robinson goes on to point out the features of these verses (*ayat*).

Firstly it is obvious that the original is characterized by rhyme. In fact the whole of the Qur'an is in rhyming prose or uses assonance. Rhyme and assonance are the basis for the division of the suras (Arabic word for chapters) into *ayahs* (Arabic word for verses, literally meaning 'sign'). Second, although these five *ayahs* are of unequal length, there is a marked rhythm. The easiest way to appreciate this is by counting the number of oscillations per line and then the structure becomes clear:

12 i.u^2
10 i.u
8 i.u
10 i.u
12 i.u

Thus there is a rhythmic symmetry, with the fifth *ayah* counterbalancing the first, and the fourth counterbalancing the second.[3]

In short, the Qur'an was not written to be read quietly by an individual as private literature, but to be chanted as part of communal worship and heard by the congregation as an act of reverence. The Christian Arab priest, Reverend Mitri Raheb, outlines the similar role played by scriptures in Judaism and Christianity:

> The word Qur'an denotes something which is recited, words that are spoken aloud and a message that is chanted. In its Semitic context, this concept of *qur'an* appears to derive from an Aramaic precedent, where the term *qeryana* denoted any biblical text sung as a part of the liturgy of the Syrian Church. A parallel concept is found in the Jewish rabbinical literature in what Hebrew calls *miqra*. This is used in the Talmud to refer to the whole Jewish Bible, serving to underline both the vocal manner of study and the central role of the public reading of scriptures played in the liturgy of the Jews. This suggests a concept of the way the Bible functions in worship that differs greatly from contemporary (especially Protestant) practices in the West. Research has shown that the concept of scripture being read silently by the individual is a recent phenomenon. There is substantial evidence that the Bible has become a silent object in Western worship. The Biblical practice that the prophet Muhammad would have been familiar with in indigenous Jewish and Christian liturgies was a community book which was chanted in worship.[4]

All of this goes to show how literary structures in Arabic enable oral traditions to pass on with great accuracy from generation to generation. Jesus used the same structures as a way of making his stories 'sticky' thus enabling his

Aramaic speaking audiences (who were largely unschooled, rural villagers) to remember and pass on accurate renditions of his teachings. I will highlight Jesus' genius as a poet throughout this book.

On several occasions in the UAE and in Kuwait, I was privileged to attend events in which poetry or the Qur'an was recited in Arabic. While I did not understand the meaning of the words, I did understand the emotional impact they had on the audience. Whether moved to tears or gently sighing in agreement or wonder, it is impossible not to be moved by the power of Arabic rhetoric delivered in a powerful and emotive environment. I have seen rich and powerful sheikhs weeping because of the words of the orator standing in front of them. I witnessed an elderly man silence a busy majlis by reciting poetry. It is difficult for me as a Westerner to understand the impact of the Arabic language; in English speaking countries it is rare to have hundreds of people turn out to listen to a night of poetry.

Christine Mallouhi recorded her experience of listening to an Arab poet:

> The artist was reciting a famous poem by one of the great mystic-philosophers, Ibn Arabi, and cleverly throwing in some unexpected comments which kept the crowd glued to him. At every beloved line or quip the crowd let out one long verbalized sigh, the famous Arab 'aaaah'. The 'aaaah' is a syllable expressing such deep and beautiful emotions from the centre of the heart it cannot be limited by a word. It's an emotive sigh. I will always remember those families and the hundreds of men of all ages, spellbound by beautiful poetry.[5]

Was it the power and eloquence of his words how Jesus was able to draw crowds? That along with his healing ministry would have made him a 'must see' for the local people.

Christian Arabs have continued to retell the teachings of Jesus in Arabic poetry since pre-Islamic times. Bishop Kenneth Cragg, a well-known British scholar of Islam and Arabic and a former Bishop of Jerusalem and Iran, lists some of the great esteemed poets who were widely renowned for their poetry. These included:

> Poets at the courts of the *Ghassanids* and the *Lakhmids* in the times before Islam... whose poems ruminate on life and death and courage in a Christian strain. One of the greatest Christian poets was Al-Nabhani who belonged to the *Tayy* tribal grouping in the north of Najd which appears to have been in touch with the Ghassanids farther north. Their territory was on the eastern flank of the pilgrim route to Mecca.[6]

It is quite possible that the prophet of Islam would have met some of the Christian Arab tribes during his merchant days and would have heard some of this poetry. Later on, during the rapid expansion of the Islamic empire, the Christian tribes of the Ghassanids and Lakhmids rode with the triumphant Muslim army and helped end the Byzantine and Persian grip on Arabian land. Along the way there would have been an exchange of poetry and stories, providing fertile soil for an exchange of ideas and beliefs. The key to all of this is the language of the Arabs which lends itself to rhythm and rhyme. This is the oral environment in which Jesus was raised.

JESUS THE POET

What is less appreciated is that Jesus was a master poet who employed clear structures and styles in presenting his stories and parables. Kenneth Bailey breaks down Jesus' teaching about the Good Shepherd to show clearly how Jesus used poetical and narrative devices to ensure that his teachings were preserved in an oral tradition.

1a.	I am the good shepherd.	*Good Shepherd*
1b.	The good shepherd lay down his life for his sheep.	
2.	He who is a hireling and not a shepherd, Whose own the shepherd are not.	*Hireling*
3.	Sees the wolf coming.	*Wolf – comes*
4.	and leaves the sheep and flees.	*Hireling – flees*
5.	and the wolf snatches them and scatters them.	*Wolf – snatches*
6.	He flees because he is a hireling. And cares nothing about the sheep	*Hireling*
7a.	I am the good shepherd. I know my own and my own know me, As the Father knows me and I know the Father	*Good Shepherd*
7b.	and I lay down my life for the sheep.[7]	

Bailey notes the use of seven 'movements' or steps in the structure (the number seven being a very significant number in Jewish thought) and the 'sandwich' structure of the teaching, which begins with the theme of the Good Shepherd and ends with the same theme. To the listener and the reader, the structure of the poetry leads them to conclude that the concept of Shepherd is the thrust or the focus of the poem. Attention then is drawn to the idea of Jesus stating that he is a 'good shepherd'. Thus the ingredients of this seven layer sandwich parable are:

1. GOOD SHEPHERD
2. HIRELING
3. WOLF
4. HIRELING
5. WOLF
6. HIRELING
7. GOOD SHEPHERD

What is the message of this parable? The pastoral imagery of a shepherd is one of the most benign and comforting pictures of Jesus that is held by Christians. It is a motif that would seem inoffensive and harmless. It is a surprise then to find out that the picture of a shepherd is anything but! The next chapter explores how Jesus' audience would have responded to his message and examines the theological context and historical background to his claim that he is the good shepherd.

---

1   See M. Gladwell on the importance of the 'sticky' concept in creating a mass movement.
2   An i.u. refers to an isochronic unit. Each short vowel is counted as one i.u., and a long vowel is counted as 2 i.u.s. This is a device used to measure the rhythms of poetry.
3   N. Robinson, *Discovering the Qur'an: A Contemporary Approach to a Veiled Text* (London: SCM,1996), p.10.
4   Dr Mitri Raheb, *Sailing through Troubled Waters: Christianity in the Middle East* (Bethlehem: Diyar Publisher, 2013), pp. 60–61.
5   C .A. Mallouhi, *Waging Peace on Islam* (London: Monarch Books, 2000), p. 196.
6   Kenneth Cragg, *The Arab Christian: A History in the Middle East* (Kentucky: John Knox Press, 1991), p. 258.
7   Kenneth Bailey, *Jesus Through Middle Eastern Eyes: Cultural Studies in the Gospels* (London: SPCK), p. 368.

SHEPHERD

JESUS REFERRING TO HIMSELF as the good shepherd would have been a very provocative statement in the historical and religious cultural environment of the time. While the shepherd motif was occasionally employed to describe kings and religious leaders, the most enduring use in Scripture is its application for describing God and His relationship with His people. This is a theme which runs from Genesis through to the Psalms and the main prophets.[1] Psalm 23 is the best-known one, beginning with 'The LORD is my shepherd'. They all describe a God who will lead and guide his people and protect them from danger. The Old Testament then makes several 'predictions' or prophetic statements about the nature of the Messiah. The Messiah is a Biblical figure descended from King David who will be sent by God to usher in a new era bringing God's presence, and hope to the peoples of the earth. These prophecies also refer to the Messiah as a shepherd. Thus Ezekiel prophesied that 'My servant shall be King over them; and they shall all have one shepherd' (Ezekiel 37:24).

Jesus appropriates this imagery and applies it to himself. To his contemporary listeners this was an outrageous statement. Imagery which was regarded as sacred and divine was being hijacked to describe the identity of a man whom most regarded and knew as the son of a carpenter. The implications of Jesus' teachings are very clear, even if we might not agree with them. Jesus states baldly that he is a divine figure sent to bring the sheep home. The title of the good shepherd highlights not just his role but also his identity. Jesus once explained that 'only God is good' (Mark 10:18).

Using a highly stylized teaching method, Jesus rams his point home with the beginning of his declaration that he is the 'good shepherd' with the last line reinforcing his opening statement. It was startlingly bold.

Kenneth Bailey analyzed the linguistic structures underlying the teachings of Jesus. His research demonstrated that Christ consistently used poetic rhetorical devices to help his listeners remember and recall his messages with ease.[2] The parable of the Good Shepherd is a powerful example of Jesus using poetry to convey his teaching.

PERSONAL OBSERVATIONS ON THE SHEPHERD THEME

He calls his own sheep by name and leads them out... I am the good shepherd. The good shepherd lays down his life for his sheep... I know my sheep and my sheep know me.

– John 10:14, 11, 14

The Biblical culture and world view present in the Middle East really struck me when I served as a youth worker for a church in Derbyshire. I had spent a few years living in the Middle East prior to that and I had travelled extensively through town and desert. I remember clearly the day when

I realized that Christians in the West were really missing so many layers of understanding when they read their scriptures because they had not lived in the Middle East or the Gulf region. Living in that part of the world had brought so many stories in Scripture to life for me. The sights, smells, and the humdrum of daily Arab life was rooted in a culture which seemed to have changed little in substance since the days of Jesus.

I was driving on a small winding country road headed towards a village called Brassington. It was a glorious day and as the quaint village came into view in the distance, I saw out of the corner of my eyes activity in a field. It was a shepherd working with two dogs. As I was early for my appointment, I pulled the car over and sat on the wall to watch them at work.

Using signals and whistles, the shepherd skilfully commanded the dogs to drive the loosely scattered sheep into a tight huddle. The dogs stalked, menaced, and occasionally snapped at the sheep in order to force them to go in the right direction. The sheep were driven forwards, compelled by the fear of the dogs that were relentless in pursuing them and pressing in beside them. It was an engaging spectacle and I remember contemplating the scene with great satisfaction. I was musing on the words of Jesus when he described himself as the good shepherd.[3]

'Wait a moment!' I thought to myself. Something jarred with the scene before me and the comforting ambience of the imagery I associated with Jesus. One of the dogs barked and a startled sheep ran in the direction of the others.

For the sheep in England, a shepherd is not someone they associate with security and lovey-dovey feelings. A shepherd is someone who sets the dogs on them. The English shepherd makes you go somewhere you really do not want to go using menace and fear in the form of barks, growls, and teeth. The contrast then with a shepherd

I saw in the Middle East some years earlier couldn't have been greater.

I was in Jordan, wandering along a dirt track near a camp in the rolling hills of Gilead. Ahead of me I heard the sound of singing and as I rounded a bend, I saw a young shepherd. He was ambling along the track and behind him shuffled a loose herd of sheep. Any sheep that dawdled and spent too long grazing soon drew the attention of the shepherd. He called out to the sheep by name, startling it, but provoking it to move along in the direction of the shepherd.

I remember another encounter with a shepherd in Kuwait. We were living in the oil town of Ahmadi, and one day as I came out of my bungalow, I was scandalized to see a large sheep eating the flowers in my garden. After futile efforts to shoo the sheep off my premises (providing huge entertainment for my wife and children who were watching through the window), a shepherd boy suddenly materialized at the gate. One call to the sheep solved my dilemma, and I watched in some disbelief as the sheep obediently trotted off after the shepherd.

One of the most famous passages of scripture is Psalms 23. Sung or read at countless funerals it is familiar to generations of English people. But what image is really going through their minds when they hear this? Is it the one formed by their own culture or is it the Middle Eastern shepherd, which the original author of Psalms intended to share with us?

> The Lord is my shepherd
> I shall not be in want
> He makes me lie down in green pastures
> He leads me beside quiet waters
> He restores my soul
> He guides me in paths of righteousness
> for his name's sake.

Even though I walk through the valley
of the shadow of death
I will fear no evil for you are with me
Your rod and your staff they comfort me.

— Psalm 23

Do you see an English shepherd there? Where are the dogs? This passage appears to describe a familiar image in the Middle East.

The most comforting aspect of a Middle Eastern shepherd is that he walks ahead of the sheep. The second aspect missed is the intimacy the shepherd has with his sheep. They are familiar with his voice and he knows their names.

The sheep go to a place where the shepherd has already been and gone on ahead. He calls them to follow him and trust him. The ambience of security and safety is familiar. The meaning of this pastoral imagery is obvious to a Middle Eastern audience. To a western audience the image of the shepherd needs to be spelled out.

Wherever you go in life, whatever the circumstances you find yourself in, no matter what crisis befalls you, the shepherd has already been there ahead of you. Even if you walk through the valley of the shadow of death, He is ahead of you, leading the way.

Westerners may well have a picture of God or of Jesus which relates more to the image of an English shepherd. That is a bully who drives people through fear and control. That image of God would really shape a person's whole relationship with God and tarnish any religious experiences. They may literally feel the hounds driving them into an unknown destiny which may or may not be benign.

Theologians describe the shepherd imagery as *pastoralia*. The very term 'pastor', describes the shepherding function of a church leader. This reflects the teaching of the scriptures which describes God in quite intimate terms. God is like a shepherd and we are His sheep. Drawing upon this scriptural motif, Jesus intuits that his own ministry and identity is a manifestation of the divine shepherd.

---

1   Genesis 49:24; Psalms 77:20, 79:13, 80:1, 95:7, 100:3; Ezekiel 34:22; Jeremiah 31:10, 50:19; Isaiah 40:11; Micah 2:12-13.
2   Kenneth Bailey, *Poet & Peasant and Through Peasant Eyes* (Michigan: Eerdmans, 1983).
3   John 10:11

BREAD

Jesus said, 'For the bread of God is the bread who comes down from heaven and gives life to the world.'... Then Jesus declared, 'I am the bread of life. Whoever comes to me will never go hungry, and he who believes in me will never be thirsty.'

– John 6:33–35

THIS CHAPTER EXAMINES THE cultural and theological significance in Jesus' teaching about bread. It also highlights his use of rhetorical devices to enable his teachings to be memorable and passed on in a reliable oral form.

Bread is the staple diet in the Gulf. It is not only a food item to be consumed, but it is also used as cutlery, to scoop and shovel food into our mouths. Bread can be used as a plate, a 'mop up' cleaner and it is found in every home, even the very poorest. It even features in the most famous prayer that Jesus ever taught, 'Give us this day our daily bread' (Luke 11:2–4).

The American Lebanese chef, Habeeb Salloum, explains the role of bread across the Arabian peninsula:

> Arabs, the majority people in the Middle East, eat bread
> with every meal. In tradition and in daily life, bread is held

to be a divine gift from God. The Egyptians call bread
'aysh' which means 'life itself.' In the Arab world, if a piece
of bread falls on the floor, a person will pick it up and
kiss it, then eat it. I used to see this happen at home
when my mother dropped a piece of bread on the floor,
not allowing it to be thrown away with the garbage.

The Spanish picked up this habit from the Arabs during
their long stay in the Iberian Peninsula. In Spain, when
a piece of bread falls on the floor, in the Arab fashion they
will say: '*Es pan de Dios*' (in Arabic, *'aysh Allah'* means
God's bread).

The Arabs claim that they cannot taste other foods without
bread and the bread types they have to choose from are
numerous and varied. Arab bread comes in many textures,
sizes, and shapes. Without question, the mother of all
these Middle Eastern breads is pita – by far, the most
popularly found in the Middle East, called *Khubz Arabee*
among the Arabs.[1]

It is interesting to see how bread is so closely identified
with life and God. Way back in Middle Eastern history, we
read of the use of bread being displayed as a symbol of the
presence of God in the great temple.[2] Placed in the Holy of
Holies, the *shew* bread was the symbol that directly represented the life and presence of God. Bread was also one of
the things that the people were called to sacrifice to God in
order to purify their priests.[3]

Could it be that the Middle Eastern respect for bread
today harkens back to the time when bread was placed at
the heart of the temple of Jerusalem?

What is disturbing to the Middle Eastern mind familiar
with the symbol of bread being used to signify the divine,
is that Jesus clearly seems to identify himself with this

symbol. 'I am the bread of life' is a claim that would only be understood by his listeners as a blasphemous statement; that is, Jesus was claiming to be God. That the crowds interpreted the teachings of Jesus in this way is demonstrated through their anger in response to his words and seeking to stone him to death. This self-understanding of Jesus is one of the points of debate between Christians and Muslims, yet this is not an isolated example of a teaching of Jesus in which he seemingly identifies his personhood with God.[4]

Bread is also a symbol of hospitality. Witness how Jesus uses the following story about bread to make a powerful spiritual point:

> Then Jesus said to them, 'Suppose you have a friend, and you go to him at midnight and say, "Friend, lend me three loaves of bread; a friend of mine on a journey has come to me, and I have no food to offer him."
>
> And suppose the one inside answers, "Don't bother me. The door is already locked, and my children and I are in bed. I can't get up and give you anything." I tell you, even though he will not get up and give you the bread because of friendship, yet because of your shameless audacity he will surely get up and give you as much as you need.
>
> 'So I say to you: ask and it will be given to you; seek and you will find; knock and the door will be opened to you. For everyone who asks receives; the one who seeks finds; and to the one who knocks, the door will be opened.'
>
> – Luke 11:5–10

Again, Jesus is displaying his skill as a consummate storyteller and poet in an oral tradition. Bailey highlights the structure underpinning this story in what he terms,

The Parable of the Friend at Midnight. He identifies two groups of stanzas containing six lines each. Each stanza 'inverts', meaning that the first and sixth line are parallel in theme, then line two and five complement one another with lines three and four providing the pinnacle of the main thrust of the story. Bailey maps out the story as follows:

Stanza A (What will not happen)

And he said to them,
'Can any one of you imagine
having a friend
and going to him at midnight,

1. And saying to him,   *Request*
    'Friend, lend me three loaves

2. for a friend of mine   *Reason for request*
    has arrived on a journey

3. And I have nothing   *Appeal to duty*
    to set before him.'

4. And will he answer   *Duty refused*
    from within,
    'Don't bother me!

5. The door is now closed   *Reason for refusal*
    and my children
    are in bed with me.

6. I cannot get up   *Request refusal*
    and give you anything.'

Stanza B (What will not happen)

'I tell you,
1. Though he will not   *Request refused*
    give him anything

2. Having arisen   *Arise*

3. Not because   *Not for the sake*

	of being his friend	*of friendship*
4.	But because of	*For the sake*
	his avoidance of shame	*of honour*
5.	He will get up	*Arise*
6.	And give him	*Request granted*
	whatever he wants'[5]	

Bailey correctly highlights that the theme of this story centres on giving because it is the honourable thing to do in the culture of Jesus' listeners. The rhetorical question at the beginning of the story, 'Can you imagine... ?' is written in such a way where the obvious and expected answer would be 'No!'. Every Middle Easterner could not imagine not helping their friend fulfil his code of hospitality as they know his honour is at stake. To not get up to help his friend would be inexcusable. So what is the point of this story?

The context of this story is that Jesus is teaching about prayer. The disciples have seen Jesus praying and they want to learn from him. So they asked him to give them a lesson on how to pray. In response to this, Jesus teaches them the prayer, which we now know as the Lord's Prayer or the 'Our Father'. This prayer contains several specific requests which are all quite profound when examined. These are the words which Jesus taught:

> Father, hallowed be your name, your kingdom come.
> Give us each day our daily bread. Forgive us our sins,
> for we also forgive everyone who sins against us. And
> lead us not into temptation.
>
> – Luke 11:2–4

So he teaches his followers to ask for the following things:

'Your kingdom come.' In other words, the one praying is requesting that God rules in their lives as though they were living in his presence in heaven.

'Give us each day our daily bread.' This can be interpreted literally. Bread was the daily sustenance and the
primary diet of the people. We can also read into it a more
fundamental demand, which would equate to, 'Give us
life', or, 'Meet out our basic needs'. It is an acknowledge-
ment of the conviction of the Middle Easterner that bread
equals life.

'Forgive us our sins.' This request acknowledges a
widespread human condition that most people carry with
them a sense of guilt or anger about times when they made
mistakes. The request is tied into a condition that the one
praying is forgiven as they would forgive others.

This is an extraordinary request. Let us remember the
Middle Eastern context of this prayer. Jesus teaches this at
a time when religious law insisted that only God could forgive and that forgiveness required sacrifice. Forgiveness
was not cheap and the sacrifice was usually the life of a
pigeon, a sheep, or an ox (the animal sacrificed depended
on the wealth of the petitioner and a sense of the scale of
forgiveness required).

Here, the sacrifice required for God's forgiveness is that
we in turn learn to forgive others in order to experience
the liberation of being forgiven. Failure to forgive others
has been well documented by psychologists as having a
detrimental effect on our mental health. This is quite contrary to the requirements of religious law. If a neighbour
had wronged you, it demanded retribution. The blood feud
was sanctioned in scripture and the only exemption from
immediate justice for a murderer was if the guilty fled to
certain appointed cities of sanctuary. There they could be
sure of some form of protection until there was a proper
investigation into the circumstances surrounding the
death. Even then, forgiveness required sacrifice.

Jesus was teaching his Middle Eastern disciples to move
away from the blood feud and instead seek forgiveness

from God based on their ability to offer human forgiveness. This is incredibly difficult, but the implications for a society rife with blood feuds and lack of forgiveness is deeply radical. In effect, this prayer request is calling upon God to change our fundamental desire for revenge and, in doing so, set us free from the vicious cycle of hatred and retribution.

'Lead us not into temptation.' The final request is a plea for God's protection and the ability to make choices in life that will keep us out of trouble and destruction. This is a deliberate request for God to intervene in guiding us in our decision making, especially in the realm of morality and ethics.[6]

Having taught the Lord's Prayer, Jesus then goes straight into the story of the persistent neighbour asking for bread from his friend. In doing so, he links the prayer and the story together to make a powerful statement about how prayer works.

His parable highlights that persistence (nagging or pestering may be better words) paid off for the neighbour. His friend gave him bread not because he was close to him, but because he knew he had to honour the reputation of his friend's hospitality (and his own). This involved the considerable inconvenience of getting up in the dark, untangling himself from the limbs of his sleeping children and wife (they usually all slept on the floor in one room), exiting the house, crossing the courtyard over to the main heavy gate set in the outer wall, and then addressing the needs of his neighbour. The neighbour nonetheless got his bread because the alternative was to bring shame on his friend and himself. Jesus teaches that is how we pray. We pester God! We pursue him for our daily needs. We demand that he acts in our lives as though we were in heaven already! The implication is that God will uphold the honour of his name so that we will not be shamed.

To drive home this very concept of honour and shame being linked to prayer, Jesus teaches the following immediately after challenging his disciples to ask, seek, and knock:

> Which of you fathers, if your son asks for a fish, will give him a snake instead? Or if he asks for an egg, will give him a scorpion? If you then, though you are evil, know how to give good gifts to your children, how much more will your Father in heaven give the Holy Spirit to those who ask him!
>
> – Luke 11:11–13

The examples Jesus quotes in this last passage seem rather random. Bailey makes sense of this by quoting an Arab commentator on the Gospels:

> Bread, fish and eggs are the ordinary food of a common man... A round stone looks like a round loaf, and there is little outward difference between the snake of the sea (which is a kind of fish) and a snake of the land which is an ordinary snake... and the scorpion all folded up looks like an egg.[7]

Again this whole teaching is presented in a poetical structure. Highlighting Jesus' skill as an orator and the Middle Eastern oral tradition in which he was steeped. Bailey demonstrates the literary form:

Stanza A

      And to you I say
1.   Ask. And it shall be
      given to you
2.   Seek, and you shall find   *(2nd person)*

3. Knock and it shall be
    opened to you.
1. For everyone who asks receives
2. And the one who seeks finds   (*3rd person*)
3. And to the knocker `
    it shall be opened

Stanza B

   And will anyone of you
1. If the son asks the father for bread
2. Will he give him a stone?
    1. Or a fish instead of a fish?
    2. Will he give him an eel (snake)?
    3. or if he asks an egg
    4. will he give him a scorpion?

Stanza C

   If therefore
4. You being evil
5. You know good gifts   (*2nd person*)
6. To give to your children
4. How much more the father
5. Out of heaven   (*3rd person*)
6. Will give the Holy Spirit
    to those asking him.

The first stanza is a clear example of step parallelism.
The pattern is: ask, seek, knock – ask, seek, knock.
The present tense of the imperatives imply continued
action and can be translated, 'keep on asking, seeking,
knocking'. The emphasis of 'anyone', which is reinforced
in the Old Syriac, can be seen as an appeal to the

outcasts; even they will receive if they ask. It could also be spoken in defense of the universality of the Gospel. Jesus could be saying to the religious people of his day, 'Everyone who asks will receive, even sinners, not just theso-called righteous'.

The second stanza contains three double images and are described as 'brief antithetical parallelisms'. Each of the couplets has the same message. A son will unfailingly receive from his father and the gift will be good.

The third stanza mirrors the first and is also a clear step parallelism. So the overall summary of the three stanzas in terms of their content is portrayed as:

Stanza A – all will receive

Stanza B – all will receive and the gift will be good

Stanza C – the gift will be good

The images of the second stanza are simple and striking. They are constructed so that even if the listener only remembers one of them, it is enough.[8]

The message is strikingly Middle Eastern. Jesus is essentially saying that God is good, like a good human father, and that the heavenly Father identifies with and understands the Arabian culture of shame and honour. He will answer prayer in order to honour His own name.

The message is simply and powerfully conveyed and demonstrates that Jesus was truly a master of the oral tradition. Jesus inhabited the world of Middle Eastern poetry and storytelling and his genius is that, centuries after his ascension, the stories are still told.

1   http://www.backwoodshome.com/articles2/salloum135.html. Issue #135, May/June, 2012 Accessed 28th July 2013.
2   Exodus 25:30 and Hebrews 9:1–5
3   Exodus 29:23–25
4   See Appendix D for a fuller discussion on the identity of Jesus.
5   Kenneth Bailey, *Poet & Peasant and Through Peasant Eyes* (Michigan: Eerdmans, 1983), p. 120.
6   There is a similar prayer in Islam in which the devout pleads with God to lead them in 'the straight way', that is, to not be led to temptation. This is found in Sura 1:6–7: 'Show us the straight way, the way of those on whom Thou hast bestowed Thy Grace, those whose (portion) is not wrath, and who go not astray'.
7   *Poet & Peasant and Through Peasant Eyes*, pp. 136–137.
8   Ibid. pp. 135–139.

RUN

There was a man who had two sons. The younger one said to
his father, 'Father, give me my share of the estate.' So he divided
his property between them. Not long after that the younger son
got together all he had, set off for a distant country and there
squandered his wealth in wild living. After he had spent everything,
there was a severe famine in that whole country and he began to
be in need. So he went and hired himself out to a citizen of that
country, who sent him to his fields to feed pigs. He longed to fill
his stomach with the pods that the pigs were eating, but no one
gave him anything. When he came to his senses, he said, 'How
many of my father's hired servants have food to spare, and here
I am starving to death! I will set out and go back to my father and
say to him: Father, I have sinned against heaven and against you.
I am no longer worthy to be called your son; make me like one of
your hired servants.' So he got up and went to his father. But while
he was still a long way off, his father saw him and was filled with
compassion for him; he ran to his son, threw his arms around him
and kissed him.

– Luke 15:11–20

G ULF ARABS DON'T RUN. It is extremely rare to see an
adult Arab anywhere in the Gulf run in public. Not
in the street, shopping malls, or anywhere. The
reason for this is quite simple. It's very difficult to run with

an abaya on, or with a *kandura* or dishdasha. Your stride is restricted by the length of the robes. The only way to break out into a full sprint is to hitch up your robes or your dress, thus allowing you to run without impediment.

This would be unthinkable in the Middle East. In a culture where revealing too much flesh is regarded as immodest and shameful it is no wonder that modest clothing is seen as a sign of virtue. To run would be undignified. To run means to show flesh and embarrass your neighbours and yourself. Running is just not respectable. It has been like this in the Middle East for a long time. The more status and standing you have in society, the less likely you are to run. This is especially true if you are a patriarchal figure, a leader of a tribe or large family, or a landowner.

Jesus tells a story where the unthinkable happens. A respectable elder father figure runs in public.

This parable is probably one of the best known stories told by Jesus. Again it is told with the use of a poetical device. Bailey describes the form of the parable of the prodigal son as a type D (parabolic ballad) which in this case has twelve stanzas that match each other using inverted parallelism. Thus the outline looks like the following:

1. A son is lost
2. Goods wasted
3. Everything lost
4. The great sin
5. Total rejection
6. A change of mind
6. An initial repentance
5. Total acceptance
4. The great repentance
3. Everything gained
2. Goods used in joyful celebration
1. A Son is found.[1]

Such a clear structure aids a culture steeped in oral tradition to remember the story outline. Bailey also highlights another structure embedded in the story, thus making it doubly 'sticky' for remembrance. He calls this structure a thematic step parallelism. This can be seen as follows:

Speech A (The first six stanzas)

He leaves
In need but unrepentant
Becomes a pig herder
Eats nothing
Is dying

Speech B (The second six stanzas)

He returns
In need and truly repentant
Becomes an honoured son
Feeds on fatted calf
Is alive.[2]

The genius of Jesus as a storyteller is revealed when we look at the underlying literary structures of his parables. He gave his audiences poetical 'hooks' which allowed them to retain and rehearse his teachings. In the parable of the prodigal son, we read the story of a young man who violated every code of good behaviour. He demanded his inheritance from his father; in other words, he wanted what would be given to him upon the death of his father.

Kenneth Bailey was curious to see what modern Middle Easterners would make of the son's request of his inheritance from his father. He asked different people all around the Middle East what would be the response to such a request. Invariably, the dialogue was as follows:

'Has anyone made such a request in your village?'
'Never!'
'Could anyone ever make such a request?'
'Impossible!'
'If anyone did, what would happen?'
'His father would beat him, of course!'
'Why?'
'This request means – he wants his father to die!'³

The care of parents was a primary duty for sons. They were under obligation to care for the elderly parents and ensure that they were respectably buried. To abandon this care of duty was a shameful action and would have brought wide condemnation from the community.

What is astonishing then, about the beginning of this parable, is that the father is so peaceful and graceful in his response. As we see from the survey above, most Arabs would expect the response to such a request to be outrage followed by a beating. The father does not respond like that at all. As Sa'id, an Oriental patriarch priest and scholar of the old school, comments:

The actions the father takes in this story are unique, marvellous, divine actions, which have not been done by any father in the past.⁴

Sa'id sensed that the actions of the father are special. The father is still an earthly father and is believable. At the same time he demonstrates qualities of love beyond what is experienced and expected from any earthly father.

The story then follows the fortunes of the young man. His money is soon squandered until finally he ends up eating the food of animals and realizes that even the servants in his own home have a better life than he. He decides to return home and is rehearsing what to say to his father.

In the meantime, the father is anxiously scanning the horizon every day. He yearns for his rebellious son to return. Then one day in the distance he sees a distant figure shuffling towards the village. As he strains his eyes he recognizes that this broken, almost unrecognizable figure, is indeed his son.

Then he does the unthinkable. He runs.

The old man hitches up his robes – exposing his legs in a most undignified and unseemly way. He races the length of the village. Everyone who saw him must have been shocked. This influential landowner, a pillar of society, abandons his respectability. All he can think about is welcoming the son home. His complete focus is to embrace his lost son to his bosom.

The same son who walked out on him. The same son who wounded him so callously by implying he wanted to live as though the old man was already dead.

Meanwhile, the son is trudging up the street, fearful of his reception, hoping beyond hope that his father might take him back as a lowly servant.

Then there is a loud shout. A cry, A blurring of arms; A deep, unexpected hug which conveys a completely scandalous message: mercy, grace, love, forgiveness. It must have been overwhelming. It should have been anger, judgment, and wrath. The humiliation, the loss of face, the burning shame, the loss of respect became not that of the son. But instead was owned by the father. Because he ran.

This story contains a powerful cultural shock which, like a sting from the scorpion's tail, would stun an Arabian audience. The father figure deliberately shamed himself out of love for his son. He made himself weak and undignified. Shame and honour were cast aside in the cause of joyful reconciliation. It is in this story we see a core theme running throughout many of Jesus' parables. Once we were lost – but now we are found.

OTHERS WHO RAN

Do we find other instances in the Gospels of other people running? Is this culturally significant? One notable incident is recorded at the end of all the Gospels. The followers of Jesus who had walked with him throughout his ministry, his teachings, his healing encounters, his suffering and death, ended up either running from the burial place of Jesus or to it.

We read about the early witnesses to the empty tomb of Jesus. The women went there to prepare the body for embalming. They left that tomb running. Adult women, hitching up their dresses, running in public. Something made them run. Something caused them to forget about dignity and shame. They simply ran.

What would make an Arab lady run? I guess they run for the same reasons as anyone else – to get somewhere in a hurry or to get away from something in a hurry. But it would have to be fairly urgent for them to run down the road in public. The only time I can think of women running in public is when they are deliberately exercising or enacting part of the *Haj* ritual, where they run in Mecca between two small hills. In this part of the *Haj*, Muslims re-enact the desperation of Hagar as she searches for a water supply for herself and her son, Ishmael. In this case, Hagar's running was due to the urgent need to find a source of life.

Some Muslim commentators are struck by the fact that the Gospel accounts of the resurrection of Jesus highlight that it is women who were the first to witness the empty tomb.[5] This is noteworthy because then as now, the religious law states that testimony of one man is equivalent to the testimony of two or four women. The commentators suggest that if the story of the resurrection is to be credible, it would have been so much better if the first witness had been a man of some repute and status. Sometimes the stories of Jesus highlight a radical departure from normal culture and this seems to be one of those instances. In some ways this makes the historical veracity of the Gospels more likely. Surely, if this was a fictional account, the author could have come up with a better witness!

While we are on the subject of the resurrection of Jesus, it is worth noting that then as now, there was scepticism surrounding the whole 'empty tomb' story.[6]

So why did those Middle Eastern women run from the tomb of Jesus? What were they feeling? Their emotions seem to have been a mix of excitement, fear, terror, and hope. They felt all of those emotions because the body of Jesus was nowhere to be found. Instead of a broken and pierced and very dead corpse, they encountered an empty tomb.

As the women burst into the place where the men were resting and hurriedly shared their news, we see another astonishing development. This time the men ran. Pulling up their robes, they raced to the tomb, and as they ducked into the gloomy cave they saw the abandoned bandages that were previously wrapped around the dead body.

The resurrection of Jesus made people run. They abandoned any thought about what the neighbours might think; they did not care about their dignity. They put all those concerns aside in order to see if the resurrection really was true. On that early morning in the rising sun, the sound of frantic running signalled new faith and hope.

---

1   Kenneth Bailey, *Poet & Peasant and Through Peasant Eyes* (Michigan: Eerdmans, 1983).

2   Ibid. p. 161.

3   Ibid. p. 162.

4   Ibid. p. 166.

5   A. Deedat, *The Choice: Islam and Christianity, Vol. One* (South Africa: Islamic Propagation Centre, 1993) and A. Thomson, *Jesus Prophet of Islam* (London: TaHa Publishers, 1977).

6   Matthew 28:11-15 describes how a story was circulated by the Jews claiming that the disciples of Jesus had stolen his body and thus promoted a false claim that the empty tomb was a miracle.

PART FIVE
THE ELEPHANT IN THE ROOM

CONCLUSION

T WO MAJOR CRITICISMS COULD be levelled at this book. The first is that the portrayal of Arabian culture found in this book is rooted in traditions from the past. In fact, this could be seen as the worst sort of Orientalism, which the Palestinian scholar Edward Said so witheringly exposed in his essay of the same name. Is the conventional image of the Arabian Gulf a skewed, somewhat romanticized ideal, which bears little resemblance to the contemporary reality? As a Western Christian leader who has little knowledge of the Arabic language, my access to and understanding of local culture is severely restricted. However, because of the widespread use of English by the local people, the fact that many Islamic resources have been translated into English (including the Holy Qur'an), and my living in the region on and off for twenty years, I have gained a substantial awareness of Arabian Gulf culture.

The modern Gulf Arab is a savvy technocrat rooted in a globalized economy to an extent where he or she often functions better in the corporate world in the language of English than in Arabic. Modern Arab men and women are familiar with global icons, media, and cultural references. For example, a recent South Korean pop (described as 'K-Pop') concert held in Abu Dhabi revealed a formidable Emirati fan base.

The English language is widely spoken across the Gulf and this leads to a niggling concern by authorities that the Arabic language is in danger of being marginalized. I was struck by this when I went to a Kuwaiti Author's book launch. He had written a book on Kuwaiti maritime history in the English language. When I asked the author why he had not written his book in the Arabic language, he told me with great pain that he wanted his Kuwaiti grandson to read it. The typical affluent, young Gulf Arab is potentially just as likely to be disconnected from the cultural world of Jesus as a teenager growing up in Manchester or Chicago is. The book, *Jesus of Arabia*, could be viewed as an anachronistic tribute to a culture, which has now changed beyond recognition.

The second major criticism is that there is no empirical research to back up the question of what the teachings of Jesus might mean to a Gulf Arab, be they the modern or the conservative sort. The contents of this book could be seen as plain speculation. This highlights the need to do a systematic study emulating the methodology of Kenneth Bailey, as mentioned in the Introduction.

Using the tools of exegesis, textual criticism, and contemporary anthropological fieldwork, and drawing on the insights from Bailey's work from the Levant, we can make an informed opinion on how the words of Jesus would resonate in a Gulf Arab state today.

If one is convinced that the Gospel is a reliable record of Jesus' teachings, then there are some clear conclusions.

The teachings of Jesus will make uncomfortable reading for anyone who is serious about understanding Jesus' mission and identity. Far from being a pious and popular teacher who espoused moral values that appealed to the masses, the reality is that his initial audiences, as described in the Gospels, were angered and scandalized by his stories.

The parables consistently communicate the same message about his identity and mission. The message is that Christ linked himself to the divine in such a way as to suggest that he was inseparably linked. To suggest that these controversial teachings were later inventions by devout followers would require a massive rewrite of all extant Gospels. To accomplish this within the lifetime of the original disciples of Jesus[1] would require absolute collusion. There is no evidence of this.

Using impressive skills of rhetoric and oratory, Jesus brought home a shocking message. He laid claim to the title of Messiah. His listeners, a deeply religious and conservative people, frequently responded (as recorded in the Gospel accounts) by accusing Jesus of blasphemy. His teachings ultimately led Jesus to a death sentence.

During his short public ministry, spanning a mere three years, witnesses testified that Jesus was not just a teacher, but he was also a healer and a worker of miracles. The Holy Qur'an, too, acknowledges this aspect of Jesus' ministry. John's Gospel describes the miracles as 'signs', that is, actions which were intended to semaphore a message in visual terms, which complemented Jesus' spoken words. The message which emerges from the Gospel accounts is that the words and actions of Jesus all point to his evident belief in himself not only as someone who was a prophet sent by God, but more than that, a person who seemed to embody God himself in his own humanity. The Gospel of John explained this:

> 'The Word became flesh and made his dwelling among us. We have seen his glory, the glory of the one and only Son, who came from the Father, full of truth and grace and truth.'
>
> – John 1:14

Such a statement seems insane. If anyone today were to stand up in a mosque or a church and declare themselves unequivocally to be God, they would cause deep offence, provoking at worst, a violent response and at best, a pitiful dismissal from their listeners. But, history has not consigned this widely revered prophetic figure to the bin of madmen and lunatics. Why not?

The Gospels portray a profoundly 'human' Jesus who radiates a morality, sanity, and integrity. The temptation to focus on this 'human' Jesus has led to movements to divest Jesus of his divine claims and instead highlight his humanity and his unique teachings on morality. This movement rejects *carte blanche* all supernatural claims attached to Jesus' ministry and seeks ways to rationalize what they describe as a late mythology, which reinvented a Jesus of 'faith' who bore no similarity to the Jesus of 'history'.[2]

In this way, Jesus is stripped down in order to be more compatible with the world view of his detractors. This has been done despite the antagonism to the 'myth' of Jesus' deity, because there is a deep resonance with the social and ethical implications of Jesus' message, which has a broad humanitarian appeal.

Yet the Gospel accounts make it difficult to separate the divine claims of Jesus from his more 'human' statements.

Another reason why Jesus has not been consigned to lunacy is the clear evidence to the contrary. His lucid reasoning and skill in debating the most learned members of his society, the respect that Pilate the Roman governor accorded him when he could not find anything to accuse him of, and the fact that he drew followers from such a wide range of society suggests that Jesus inspired and commanded conviction from those who knew him best. There are many examples of leaders throughout history who inspired loyalty through fear and control. There is no evidence that Jesus used such tactics to create loyalty.

If anything he did the opposite. He *discouraged* followers by asking them to give up their wealth, as in the story of the rich young ruler,[3] or by asking them to go on their own way, as he did with Bartimaeus who was healed of blindness, the man healed of lameness at the pool of Siloam, and the demonized man of Gadarene.[4]

The only way to resolve the tension between his sound teachings, the integrity of his character, and the outrageous claims he made with regards to his identity is to accept that maybe there is some substance to his claims. As C. S. Lewis once famously said, 'We are not left with the option of finding Jesus a good man – he must either be a liar, that would make him bad, or mad... or God'.[5] He pleaded with the reader to allow the Biblical texts to speak for themselves and to draw their own conclusions.

Throughout this book, we have looked at a selection of Jesus' teachings. I have fashioned them somewhat crudely around a cultural construct as provided by Mark Allen and in doing so attempted to connect the world of Jesus to the world of the Arabian Gulf today. In doing so, I am only scratching the surface.

What is needed now is for more opportunities for the Western church to hear how Arab readers respond to the text through the prism of their culture. One such method is being pioneered by the Cambridge Centre for Interfaith studies, led by David Ford. He developed the use of Scriptural Reasoning in which he invites groups of different faith communities to encounter the religious texts of others and to record their reactions.

Bear in mind that when we read scripture, we usually read them through an inherited tradition, which defines how we understand the texts culturally and theologically. Fresh insights are thrown up when someone without any form of 'tradition conditioning', starts to interpret what they read.

In the introduction of this book I mentioned the work of Kenneth Bailey. I described the use of two tools he sought to use to reveal the original impact of Jesus' words on his original audience. These tools were textual analysis and ethnographic interviews. Bailey examined ancient Middle Eastern texts and interviewed countless Middle Eastern villagers to get a fresh perspective on what the stories of Jesus meant to them in their culture. Bailey found a rich supply of ancient commentaries in the Egyptian Orthodox Coptic Church and the Lebanese Church. Is there a similar textual resource for the Gulf?

The answer might be a cautious 'Yes'. What is little known in the West is that there is a treasure trove of Bible commentaries from the Arabian Gulf region. Centuries ago, the Christian church flourished throughout the Arabian Gulf region. This included a monastery in Sir Bani Yas Island off the coast of Abu Dhabi in the UAE, which provided the first real evidence of the pre-Islamic Christian presence in the region. Other churches were found on Failaka island in Kuwait and in Jubail on the Eastern coast of Saudi Arabia. These were not far flung and marginalized communities, irrelevant to the life of the Church of the East. Some of the most important theologians and liturgists emerged from monastic communities based in Bahrain, Oman, Abu Dhabi, and Qatar. Of these the greatest was St Isaac of Nineveh (believed to have originated from Abu Dhabi). His spirituality made him one of the foremost writers of the entire Church of the East tradition. He remains one of the most significant theological and liturgical influences on Eastern Christian monasticism, even today.

Byzantine and Syriac church records reveal there were five bishoprics on the Western side of the Gulf. The Bishop of Sohar (Oman) and the Bishop of Qatar were signatories on the pivotal statement of Christian doctrine, the Nicene Creed, which was signed in Nicaea in the year AD 325.

In the year 676 AD, there was a regional Arabian
ecumenical council held in Darin on the island of Tarut
which was attended by George, Catholicos of the East
and Patriarch of the East; Thomas the Metropolitan
Bishop of Bet Qatraye, Iso'yahbe, the Bishop of Darin;
Sergius, the Bishop of Trihan; Stephanus, Bishop of
the Mazinuye; and other bishops from Saudi Arabia,
including Pousai (Al Hasa) and Sahin (Hatta).[6]

The Churches in the Southern part of the Gulf were orga-
nized into a region, or a Diocese, called 'Beit Qatraye', or in
modern English, 'the house of Qatar'. Priests and monks
were named after the areas from whence they came. Other
scholars include Dadisho Qatraye who is famed for being
the learned superior of the Mar Abraham Monastery and for
his writing. There is also Gabriel Qatraye who was a skilled
Biblical scholar, and Abraham Qatraye Bar Lipahis, known
for his liturgical work. Then there was Ayoub Qatraye who
wrote an introduction to the Psalter, which was utilized by
Ibn Al Tayyib (d.1043) who wrote Biblical commentaries
in Arabic. There are few in the Western Church who will
have heard of Ishpanah Qatraye, Jacob Qatraye the Bishop
of Darin, or Rabban Bar Sidhe, all of whom hailed from the
Arabian Gulf and contributed much to the theology and
practice of the church. Many of their extant works in Syriac
and Arabic have yet to be translated into English.[7] Their
Bible commentaries offer a unique insight into how the
early church in the Gulf would have understood the teachings of Jesus from an Arabian Gulf perspective. This would
be a rich seam for Biblical scholars to explore.

The second tool used by Kenneth Bailey was ethnographic interviews in which he entered rural communities in Egypt and the Levant to question elders whose way
of life had changed little over the centuries. The story of
the Omani Arabs, outlined in the opening of this book

suggests that there are cultural interpretations of the stories of Jesus that would be completely alien to a Western reading of the text – and yet these interpretations may capture the original intent of Jesus' communications.

While much of the Arabian Gulf has modernized at a breakneck pace, there are still pockets of traditional communities who boast of following a way of life, which has not changed for centuries. Following the methodology of Kenneth Bailey, it would be fascinating to see how these tradition-rich communities would respond to and interpret the parables of Jesus. As things stand, there is no published research on exploring how contemporary Gulf Arabs understand and react to the teachings of Jesus.

One tool emerging in interfaith dialogue is the use of Scriptural Reasoning. It is still a new concept in the Arabian Gulf region, but it is being used effectively in places like Oman through the Al Amana Institute, which is committed to developing best practices in interfaith relations.

Scriptural Reasoning is a form of religious dialogue spreading around the world. It was pioneered by Professor David Ford of Cambridge University, who explains the process:

> Scriptural Reasoning is the communal practice of reading sacred scriptures in small groups together. Normally the passages of scripture chosen are Jewish, Christian or Muslim and are linked by a particular issue, theme, story or image. When read together in this way participants or 'reasoners' – have found that astonishing, powerful and at times quite surprising new conversations and relationships open up.
>
> Although this practice has its origins in a university setting, and is generating considerable theoretical interest, it is also now becoming a 'civic practice'

whereby people of different faiths engage with their
holy scripture and with each other as neighbours and
fellow citizens. It is proving transformative, though
not always easy.[8]

So the final challenge of this book is this: Let us learn
from one another on how we read and interpret the
teachings of Jesus. The Western church does not necessarily
understand the Middle Eastern cultural platform from
which Jesus addressed his original audience. One way
to recover a fresh perspective is to listen to Arab voices
reading the words and actions of Jesus. For such a step to
occur, Christians first need to convince their Arab Muslim
friends that the Gospels are a good starting place to have a
dialogue. Muslims need to understand that dismissing the
Gospels as error-ridden and unreliable is both misguided
and inaccurate.

Secondly, Christians must be willing to reciprocate a
'dialogue of texts' by engaging respectfully with the Holy
Qur'an in the spirit of seeking to interpret and understand
the Islamic scriptures. In this way, Muslims might hear
fresh insights into their own sacred texts.

---

1   Most scholars agree that the Gospels were all written within thirty years of the
    death of Jesus.
2   J. Hicks, *The Myth of God Incarnate* (London: SCM Press, 1977) and A. N. Wilson,
    Jesus: A Life (New York: W. W. Norton & Company, 1992).
3   Mark 10:25
4   Mark 5:18–19
5   C. S. Lewis, *Mere Christianity* revised and enlarged edition (Harper:
    San Francisco, 2009), p. 35.
6   Andrew Thompson, *Christianity in the UAE: Culture and Heritage* (Dubai: Motivate
    Publishing, 2011), p. 56.
7   For an excellent and up-to-date overview of the Arabic Bible see Sidney Griffith,
    The Bible in Arabic: The Scriptures of the 'People of the Book' in the Language of Islam
    (Princeton: Princeton University Press, 2013).
8   David Ford, *The Promise of Scriptural Reasoning* (Oxford: Wiley-Blackwell, 2006), p. 15.

APPENDIX A
CORRUPTION OF SCRIPTURES

THE NOTION THAT THE scriptures of the Jews and the Christians have been corrupted is a critically important one. Unless the scriptural sources of the Judeo-Christian community are perceived as reliable and authentic, access to the teachings of Jesus will be limited due to the fact that Qur'anic references about Jesus relate more to his person rather than to his teachings.

Orthodox Islam teaches that there were four specific revelations of God, which were sent to humankind through very special prophets (nab'i) in the form of written words. These scriptures and their related nab'i were the Torah (the first five books of the Old Testament, namely Genesis, Exodus, Leviticus, Numbers and Deuteronomy) revealed to Moses; the Psalms (or *Zabiil*), given to King David (*Dawuud*); the Gospel (in Arabic *Al Injiil*), brought by Jesus; and the culminating, final revelation, The Holy Qur'an, given to Prophet Muhammad. The latter revelation (The Qur'an) clearly refers to the earlier scriptures as revelations from God.

So in view of the high regard for the revelations that preceded the Qur'an, where then did the accusation of corruption come from? Geoffrey Parrinder ponders this question:

> There is no suggestion in the Qur'an that the Gospel
> given to Jesus was different from the canonical Gospels
> held by Christians. This is a matter of importance
> in view of later Muslim polemic. Indeed the Qur'an
> enjoins that the 'people of the Gospel to judge by what
> God has sent down therein' (Sura 5:47). It speaks of
> the Gospel in their possession (Sura 7, 157 & 157) and
> urges them to follow the messenger spoken of in it.
> The Qur'an itself is sent down to confirm the Book,
> which was before it, and to act as a protector over
> . it (Sura 5:48)[1]

One implication of the last sura quoted then, is that if the Gospel has been corrupted, then does this mean that the Qur'an has failed in its task to safeguard the previous revelation? Clearly, the Muslim answer would be no.

So what does the Qur'an actually say on the subject of *Tahrif*, that is to change or corrupt? In sura 45, Allah says of the Jews:

> And we granted them (the Jews) clear signs in affairs of
> religion. It was only after knowledge had been granted
> to them that they fell into schisms through insolent envy
> among themselves. Verily the Lord will judge between
> them on the day of judgment as to those matters which
> they set up differences.
>
> – Sura 45:16–17

Read without commentary, the sura acknowledges that there were differences in interpretation of the Jews' revelation, which led to division and sectarianism. The Jews were of course the guardians of the Torah, yet there is nothing in the Qur'an that implies the written text itself was changed, only that the Jews had schisms amongst themselves regarding the knowledge given them.

Then of the Christians, the Qur'an reveals that, 'The sects differ among themselves; and woe to them because of the coming judgment' (Sura 19:37).

Again, read without commentary, the Qur'an exposes the regrettable state of affairs in which Christians are bitterly divided into warring sects. There is no hint that the text itself has been corrupted. Yet the persistent understanding of many Muslims is that the received texts of the Jews and Christians have been altered. Parrinder sums up the overview of Islamic opinion on this:

> Some scholars (like Biruni) declared that Jews and Christians had actually altered the text of the Bible. But others (Tabari, Ibn Khaldun, etc) said that they had interpreted the words incorrectly. It was argued that *tahrif* meant to change a thing from its original nature, but no man could possibly change words that came from God. So at the most Christians could only corrupt by misrepresenting the meaning of the word of God... In modern times some popular polemic may blame Christians for corrupting the Gospels, yet there are Muslim commentators who prefer the view that exposition has been at fault rather than any tampering with the text. Sayyid Ahmad Khan who wrote the first commentary on the Bible by a Muslim followed this viewpoint and he tried to bring Christian and Muslim exegesis into agreement. Another writer says; 'In the Koran *tahrif* means either false interpretation of the passages bearing upon Mohammed or non-enforcement of the explicit laws of the Pentateuch. As for the text of the Bible, it had not been altered... No rival text is assumed.'[2]

One of the beliefs held and taught by orthodox Islam is that the Gospel (*Injiil*) came in the form of a book. This is the book that was given to Jesus as his message of prophethood. The New Testament, with its Gospels according to Matthew, Mark, Luke, and John, seems to confirm Islamic suspicion that the Christians have lost the Gospel according to Jesus. This is not a new suspicion as the record of a conversation between the Caliph Mahdi and the Nestorian Patriarch Timothy in AD 781 proves:

> The Caliph Mahdi asks the Bishop 'Who gave you the Gospel and was it given before the Ascension[3] of Jesus?'

> The point of this is clear. If it was given before the Ascension and it can be proved that the Gospel in the hands of Christians were written after the Ascension then the books in the hands of the Christians cannot be the genuine Gospel.

> To this question, Bishop Timothy, knowing what the implication is, replies. He says that the Gospel was given before the Ascension, 'as the Gospel is the narrative of the Economy of the works and words of Jesus Christ and as the works of Christ were done and his concrete words delivered to us before his Ascension', and further if the Gospel is the preaching of the Kingdom of Heaven it certainly came before the ascension.

> But the Caliph is not prepared to let it go at that and asks whether the gospel was not written in parts by Matthew, Mark Luke and John? To which the reply is that they wrote and transmitted what they heard and saw and learned from Christ.[4]

In other words, the sage Bishop was highlighting that the Gospel was not a book but rather the message and person of Christ. This is what is recorded by the New Testament authors who were witnesses to these things.

I recall explaining this to a Muslim friend of mine in Derby and his thoughtful response was, 'Does this mean that Matthew, Mark, Luke, and John are similar to those who wrote the Hadith?'

The Hadith are the Islamic collections of sayings and actions of the prophet Muhammad that were recorded by eyewitnesses. This is in contrast to the Qur'an, which is seen as the literal dictation of God's message from heaven. It was a perceptive comment, and yet, while I acknowledged his observation, the fact is that Christians regard the Gospels as authoritative, divinely inspired scripture in the same way that Muslims regard the Qur'an as the primary source of authority for their faith.

Further confusion arose with the 'discovery' of the 'Gospel of Barnabas'. The popularity of this text in the Islamic world rests on the claim that it was written by a disciple of Jesus (the same Barnabas who travelled with St Paul in the New Testament book of Acts). This Gospel states that Muhammad, not Jesus, is the Messiah and that it was St Paul who had corrupted the original message brought by Jesus. This led to an uncritical acceptance that this must be the 'true' Gospel, which had been 'lost' by the early church.

Although the first appearance of this text was in The Netherlands in 1709, it really became popular after it was translated into Urdu in the 1960s and received the support of the iconic Pakistani Islamic revivalist Abul A'la Maududi. The English translation contains a critical commentary, and several compelling reasons were given as to why this Gospel should be dismissed as a hoax. Islamic scholars[5] dismiss the Gospel of Barnabas primarily because it contains sociological and cultural references, which date to the medieval period. Cooper gives examples:

> Such practices such as duels between rival lovers were
> a creation of medieval society, for example. There are a
> number of quotations in it from Dante who lived 1266–1321.
> Soldiers in the temple rolling wooden casks of wine are
> mentioned and wooden barrels were invented in Gaul and
> not used in the Middle East in New Testament time.[6]

Another comment must be made on the difference in the understanding of how revelation is received. In Islam, the Qur'anic revelation is understood to be a literal dictation, word by word from heaven. The language of revelation was in Arabic and thus understood to be the literal word for word message from God. This is why any interpretation of the Qur'an into any language other than Arabic is seen as 'not divine'. Muslims believe that to recite a sura from the Holy Qur'an in classical Arabic is the closest thing to coming into the presence of God.

In contrast, Christians believe that divine revelation necessarily is mediated through human agency. In the process, the message of God is inevitably shaped by the culture and language of the receiver. That said, the Christian can provide evidence that the substance of the message has remained unchanged since the original reception and that any uncertainties are carefully documented in the critical index[7] found at the bottom of most good translations of the Bible. The existence of these critical indexes in some versions of the Bible seem to confirm Muslim suspicions of *tahrif*. The Christian, though, highlights the critical index as evidence of due care of their scriptures and that in fact they serve to highlight the extraordinary faithfulness in the preservation of the teachings of Jesus. Where there are variant readings, not one of them change the substance of the message actually being passed on.

Confusion is also apparent over the multiple versions of the Bible even in the same language. Muslim friends have often shown me different English translations of the New Testament and asked my opinion for which one contains the truth! The majority of these English versions are translated from the earliest copies we have in Greek, Hebrew, and Aramaic. They seek to transmit the meaning of the message rather than a word by word rendition which would make a clunky and stilted text.

In conclusion then, *tahrif* actually refers to the practice of verbal doctrinal interpretations of the sacred texts leading to division between Jews and Christians as opposed to physical textual corruption of their scriptures. Scholarly opinion[8] testifies to the consistent preservation of Judeo-Christian scriptures.

---

1   Geoffrey Parrinder, *Jesus in the Qur'an* (London: Faber, 1965), p. 145.

2   Parrinder, pp. 146–147.

3   The Ascension of Christ refers to the belief that Christ was raised up to heaven in bodily form. The Christians believe that this took place after the death and resurrection of Christ whereas the Muslim belief holds the Ascension took place before the crucifixion. Islamic Orthodoxy acknowledges a crucifixion did occur but that it was not Jesus who perished on the cross but a substitute.

4   J. W. Sweetman, *Islam and Christian Theology: Volume 1* (London: Lutterworth Press, 1945), p. 81.

5   Some of these Islamic scholars and there views are outlined in Jacques Waardenburg, *Muslim Perceptions of Other Religions: A Historical Survey* (Oxford: Oxford University Press, 1999). See especially the section on Modern Times pp. 225–304.

6   Anne Cooper, *Ishmael: My Brother* (Bromley: MARC Europe, 1985), p. 72.

7   The critical index lists variant readings or spellings found in the earliest documents or fragments of the Gospels.

8   Nicholas Perrin, *Lost in Transmission? What We Can Know About the Words of Jesus* (Dallas: Thomas Nelson, 2007).

APPENDIX B
ISLAMIC VIEWS OF THE CRUCIFIXION

ONE OF THE POINTS of difference between Islam and Christianity is over the question of 'What happened at the crucifixion of Christ?'

The Gospels of the New Testament all dwell on the Passion (the suffering) of Christ as the climax of the story. Attention is paid to Jesus' teachings on the way to Jerusalem where, according to the Gospels, he knew full well what was awaiting him. We then read of his entry into Jerusalem, which was quickly followed by his arrest and trial in which he was found guilty of blasphemy. The Roman governor of the province, a ruthless political pragmatist called Pontius Pilate, tried to get Jesus released but in the end appeased the crowds by sentencing him to death. There is a description of the torture of Christ and then finally his painful death by crucifixion. The Gospels climax with the resurrection from the dead with Christ revealing himself to his disciples as well and truly alive.

DID JESUS DIE?

One cause of distress, if not confusion, is the Christian explanation of why Jesus died. The emphasis on the innocence of Jesus and the atonement theory (that Christ died to put right or satisfy the demands of religious law for the sake of the guilty) does not speak to the Muslim of justice. Justice is a central theme of Islam, and, quite simply, for God to allow an innocent man to take the place of the guilty does not square up with the concept of a 'just' God. Much effort then has gone into seeking an alternative narrative as to what really happened to Jesus on that fateful day, which Christians call Good Friday.

For all the significance given then to the death of Jesus by the Christian faith, the Qur'anic text is sparse when it addresses the subject. The Qur'anic account of the crucifixion contains a bald statement. The only verse in the Qur'an which directly addresses this subject says, 'They did not kill him and they did not crucify him, rather it only appeared so to them (sura 4:157).

This, on the face of it, is a straightforward denial of the crucifixion and thus explains the impasse between Christians and Muslims. However, this verse is deceptively complex and raises several questions. Todd Lawson, in his work, *The Crucifixion and the Qur'an*, highlights the diverse Islamic interpretations of the above sura throughout the centuries. He sums up the viewpoints in three categories:

1. No one is crucified.
2. Jesus was crucified, but this happened only because God decided so; it was not a result of the plotting of Jews.
3. A person other than Jesus was crucified. This was the view most widely held in the contemporary Muslim world.[1]

He cites the authoritative discussion found in the *Encyclopedia of the Qur'an*:

The Qur'anic teaching about Jesus' death is not entirely
clear cut. Three things however may be said with certainty.
First, the Qur'an attaches no salvific importance to his
death. Second, it does not mention his resurrection on
the third day and has no need of it as proof of God's
power to raise the dead. Third, although the Jews thought
that they had killed Jesus, from God's viewpoint they did
not kill him or crucify him. Beyond this is the realm of
speculation. The classical commentators generally began
with the questionable premise that sura 4:157 contains an
unambiguous denial of Jesus' death by crucifixion. They
found confirmation of this in the existence of traditional
reports about a look-alike substitute and hadiths about
Jesus' future descent. Then they interpreted the other
Qur'anic references to Jesus' death in the light of their
understanding of this one passage. If however the other
passages are examined without presupposition and
sura 4:157 is then interpreted in the light of them, it
can be read as a denial of the ultimate reality of Jesus'
death rather than a categorical denial that he died. The
traditional reports about the crucifixion of a look alike
substitute probably originated in circles in contact with
gnostic Christians. They may also owe something to early
Shi'I speculation about the fate of the Imams.[2]

So we are going to examine sura 4:157 and explore some
of the ideas mentioned above and see if there is a possible reconciliation of the Gospel account with the Qur'anic
account.

WHAT DOES THE QUR'AN IMPLY
ABOUT THE CRUCIFIXION?

Firstly, the Qur'an appears to acknowledge that there
was a crucifixion (sura 4:157) and that there is a dispute

concerning Jesus linked to this crucifixion. The denial then is not that there was a crucifixion, but rather that a specified group of people were not responsible for killing him and that it was an illusion.

So who is 'they' alluded to in the Qur'an? The context of the whole passage makes it clear that the Qur'an is talking about the Jews. Sura 4:153 is addressing the People of the Book and refers to their prophet, Moses. This leads up to the verse in question and then concludes in verse 160 with a reference to the 'iniquity of the Jews'. So the disputed verse therefore means the Jews did not kill, nor crucify him.

Historically speaking then, the Qur'an is absolutely correct. Crucifixion as a method of execution was absolutely forbidden by Jewish law and so especially was the displaying of a dead body for several days.[3] Jewish capital punishment was usually carried out by the method of stoning. The victim was buried up to his waist and then large rocks were hurled at the criminal until his body and skull had been smashed to a pulp.

Under Roman occupation, the Jews had limited rights. The Romans were the ultimate legal authority and instrument of justice. They permitted the Jews to manage their own disputes but not the right to carry out capital punishment. It was the Romans then who carried out the sentence against Jesus. The Romans were experts in the business of crucifixion, and historians testify to the horror of mile after mile of crucified victims lining the roads of the Roman Empire, a grim reminder of what happened to those who violated the *Pax Romana*.

One underlying objection to the crucifixion as mentioned earlier is that God would not allow the enemies of his prophets to triumph over his will. The underlying assumption is that the will of God cannot be undermined by mere mortals. Therefore, no man can claim that he was the one who killed the Christ, the chosen one of God, as this would imply the unthinkable, that man was able to intervene in God's plans, thus revealing that God was not almighty and all powerful.

To this point of view the Christian is sympathetic. Along with Muslims, they affirm that God's ways are higher than ours and nothing will overcome his plans and purposes. Therefore, when it comes to the crucifixion, the Christian would not see this as a 'failure' of God and that therefore mankind had power to intervene and change God's plans. Rather, Christians understand that the death of Jesus was planned and purposed by God in accordance with his divine will. In other words, God permitted and allowed this tragic event to happen for a reason. Muslims see the cross as a shameful tragedy, whereas Christians see it as a magnificent demonstration of God's compassion and mercy.

This is indeed a paradox and one in which, in all truthfulness, remains a mystery to Christians as much as to everyone else. God, the creator of the heavens and the earth, submits Himself to the indignity of execution. This understanding, however, does address the theological concern Muslims have over the apparent scenario of humans having power to contravene the will of God. Humans do not have power over God... unless God permits them.

The Gospel accounts make it clear then that the death of Jesus was not an accident, nor a random act of violence and injustice, but rather the means through which God triumphs over evil. Jesus therefore is obedient to God in following this road. We see hints of this all the way through the Gospels. For example:

> Now Jesus was going up to Jerusalem. On the way, he
> took the Twelve aside and said to them, 'We are going up to
> Jerusalem, and the Son of Man will be delivered over to the
> chief priests and the teachers of the law. They will condemn

him to death and will hand him over to the Gentiles to be
mocked and flogged and crucified. On the third day he will
be raised to life!'

— Matthew 20:17–19

The purpose of Jesus sacrifice is illustrated further in
Mark's Gospel:

For even the Son of Man did not come to be served,
but to serve, and to give his life as a ransom for many.

— Mark 10:45

And during the last supper, the final meal Jesus had
with his disciples, he clearly saw what was coming. He
had ample time and opportunity to escape. His arrest took
place in the garden on the Mount of Olives, where they
could see the guard coming to arrest him. It was dark – he
could have hidden. But he did not. Instead, he states the
following words which have been repeated faithfully by
the Christian community for hundreds of years all over
the world. In the ceremony which reenacts the last supper,
sometimes called Holy Communion, the Eucharist, or simply the Lord's Supper, the church recalls that:

He took bread, gave thanks and broke it, and gave it to
them, saying, 'This is my body given for you; do this in
remembrance of me.' In the same way after the supper, he
took the cup saying, 'This cup is the new covenant in my
blood, which is poured out for you.'

— Luke 22:19–20

Then finally, as Jesus is condemned by the Roman governor, Pontius Pilate, he says, 'You would have no power
over me if it were not given to you from above' (John 19:11).

In other words, God permitted this apparent tragedy. The Gospel witnesses to his death recorded Jesus' final moment: 'Jesus said, "It is finished." With that, he bowed his head, and gave up his spirit.' (John 19:30).

The overriding impression of the Gospel narrative is that no one made Jesus choose his path. He knew his destiny and he was the one who chose to give up his life. No one took it from him.

So one interpretation of sura 4:157 is that the Jews did not kill or crucify Jesus, for they did not have that power over him even though it appeared so. Instead the Romans executed Jesus in accordance with the power and will of God.

It is the last part of the sura that raises the most questions in terms of interpretation. These are the words translated as, 'It only appeared to them [that he had been crucified]'.

We have seen above that this last clause of could be understood to refer to the concept that humans would be able to execute a divine messenger of God. The Islamic revulsion at this idea is shared by Christians. The emphasis, therefore, is that it only *appeared* that way, but really it was the will of God all along.

However, there is another interpretation which is popular within Orthodox Islamic understandings of the crucifixion. This is known as the Substitution Theory. It addresses the belief that God would not allow an innocent man to die (especially one of his faithful prophets) and so He substituted Jesus with someone who appeared to be like Jesus. There are different opinions as to who was substituted for Jesus on the cross, but a popular candidate is Judas – the man who betrayed Jesus to the guards and therefore a suitably guilty substitute.

In this scenario then, Jesus is rescued and a victim bearing his likeness is substituted and consequently executed in his stead. The ascension of Jesus, his raising up to heaven, takes effect at this moment and now Muslims await his physical return at the end of time to implement God's judgment and rule. This idea is carried over in several English interpretations of the Qur'an:

1. Only a likeness of that was shown to them[4]
2. But he was counterfeited for them[5]
3. He was represented by one in his likeness[6]
4. Though it was made to appear like that to them[7]

What is striking about this collection of translations from the latter part of sura 4:157, is that the non-Muslim translators are very clear that a substitution has taken place whereas the most modern Muslim translation (Abdel Haleem) has retained the ambiguity of the Arabic.

This leads to a rather startling revelation. The interpretation of this verse as understanding that a substitution has taken place is in fact Christian in origin. Lawson highlights that:

A factor that is frequently overlooked in discussions of the crucifixion is the history of the negative interpretation – that is to say, the interpretation which holds that the Qur'an in 4:157 actually denies the historicity of the crucifixion of Jesus. It is important to recognize that the earliest textual evidence for such an interpretation is not Muslim at all; rather it is from the pen of none other than the last great Church Father, John of Damascus (d.749).[8]

Lawson introduced this idea in his book of heresies (He saw Islam as an errant form of Christianity). The idea of substitution was originally expressed in a heretical movement called Docetism. Lawson defines what this early Christian heresy was about:

Docetism is a word that comes from the Greek verb *dokeo*
('to seem') or noun *dokesis* ('appearance'). It describes
a view that Jesus did not suffer on the cross, but only
appeared to do so.[9]

Ironically, John of Damascus, a learned scholar who was
fluent in Arabic, passed on this negative interpretation of
sura 4:157 to the Islamic scholars.

Todd Lawson, in his book, *The Crucifixion and the
Qur'an*, did an extensive survey of Islamic commentaries on the crucifixion verse. After reviewing commentaries from the earliest times, from Abd'Allah ibn Abbas to
Tabari, through to the modern era, he came to the following conclusion:

> The Qur'an simply does not say enough on the
> subject to either confirm or deny the event (of Jesus'
> crucifixion). No single writer has succeeded in
> emphasizing sufficiently the neutrality of the Qur'an
> on the subject of the crucifixion[10] of Jesus and the
> great variety of Muslim understandings of the verse
> in question.

The great variety of Muslim understandings range from
an outright rejection that any crucifixion took place, to a
variety of substitution theories where someone else died on
the cross either as a volunteer or as a victim of punishment
by God, through to affirmation that the Jesus of history did
die on the cross.

1   Todd Lawson, *The Crucifixion and the Qur'an: A Study in the History of Muslim Thought* (Oxford: Oneworld, 2009), p. 23.
2   Jane McAufliffe (ed), *The Encyclopedia of the Qur'an* (Leiden: E. J. Brill, 2005), p. 7.
3   Deuteronomy 21:23, 'His corpse must not remain all night on the tree; you shall bury him that day. For anyone hung on a tree is under God's curse'.
4   Arberry, A. J., 1964.
5   Bell, R., 1937.

6   Sale, G.
7   Abdel Haleem, 2004.
8   Lawson, T., 2009, p. 7.
9   Ibid. p. 2.
10 Ibid. p. 18.

APPENDIX C
THE IDENTITY OF CHRIST

THE MAIN DIVISION BETWEEN Islam and Christianity boils down to the question of who Jesus is. Closely linked to this is the whole issue of the Christian doctrine of the Trinity, which insists that God exists as Father, Son, and Holy Spirit. The Muslims revere Christ as a man who served God faithfully as a prophet. The Christians, on the other hand, while affirming the Islamic view of Jesus as a great prophet, insist that Jesus is much more than a mere man. As well as a prophet, Jesus is worshipped as a divine manifestation of God himself. To the Muslim, this is a deeply offensive concept. Only God can be worshipped, and to have anything receive worship due to God alone, be it creature or object, is to commit the grave sin of *shirk* (association with God). It is considered blasphemous and idolatrous to honour Jesus as the 'Son of God', an honorific title which reeks of carnal nature. How can a man elevate his nature to that of the creator of the universe? It is too big a leap and there is genuine bafflement that Christians can subscribe to such a view.

The Qur'an has Allah interrogating Jesus about the Christian claim that Jesus is part of the divine trinity:

> Allah said: 'O Jesus Son of Mary! Did you say to mankind take me and my mother for two gods besides Allah?'

> Jesus said 'It was not mine to utter that which I had
> no right.'[1]

It is worth noting that the Qur'anic understanding of the trinity is in fact polytheism (believing in many gods), consisting of Jesus the son, who is the result of a liaison between Mary the mother and God the father. Jesus' response to the charge that he was teaching polytheism is met with a firm denial. This Islamic condemnation of polytheism is one with which the Christian would also heartily agree. First of all, the Christian is strictly monotheist (the belief that there is only one God). Secondly, Mary has never been regarded in the Christian faith as a god. She is honoured and revered as the faithful servant of God who allowed God to use her as a vehicle to give birth to Jesus as mentioned earlier in this book. Jesus is repudiating the idea that anything besides God may be worshipped. Christians worship God and nothing else.

The purpose of this chapter then is to clarify the Christian understanding of trinity which is closely related to the belief that Jesus is the divine incarnation[2] of God. This is a vital subject to explore as there is a vast gap between the beliefs of Christians and Muslims.

The Muslim believes that the Christian is essentially a pagan in the form of a polytheist who celebrates a divine family of gods. They see the worship of Christ as a divine being as a grievous heresy which evolved much later in the history of the Christian religion and thus replaced the original 'true' message and person of Christ as a devout prophet of the one God.

Islamic discourse on this subject highlights the improbability of Jesus, as a devout Jewish monotheist, promoting an understanding of himself as a deity (as much of an unthinkable horror for the Jew as for the Muslim). They also highlight that the word 'trinity' itself is nowhere to be found in the Old or the New Testament and is therefore clearly a manmade construct, which was introduced later into Christian doctrine. The Trinity, in the view of many Islamic scholars, is a later addition and amendment to the teachings of Jesus. Shalabi's view on this is expressed by Ayoub as follows:

> Christianity is a mixture of Paul's teachings and pagan ideas and rituals. He presents a comprehensive table, demonstrating that the birth, trial and resurrection of Jesus were modelled after the legends of the Buddha and pagan deities of India and the Near East.[3]

In a similar vein, Abu Zahrah identifies three causes which led to the corruption of the Christian faith. These were persecution, Neoplatonic philosophy, and the syncretistic nature of Roman religion.[4]

So how does the Christian begin to respond to these charges? To abandon Trinitarian theology would be to throw out the heart of Christian belief.

I think the first place for Christians to begin is to clarify that, like the Muslim, we believe in one God who created the heavens and the earth. The very first sura of the Qur'an has a doxology to God, which can be said by Christians wholeheartedly. The *Fatiha* (meaning 'the opening') goes as follows:

> Praise be to Allah, Lord of the Universe
> The Compassionate, the Merciful,
> Sovereign of the Day of Judgment
> You alone we worship, and to you alone we turn for help.
> Guide us to the straight path,
> The path of those whom you have favoured,
> Not of those who have incurred your wrath,
> Nor of those who have gone astray.[5]

All of the statements describing God in this most important chapter of the Qur'an (which is usually recited at the beginning of many public events) would find agreement with Christians. The Christian believes God is Lord of the Universe, that he is Love, the embodiment of mercy and compassion. The Christian also shares the view that there will be a day of judgment and that God will be Master of that time. This is the God we worship and seek guidance from.

The Christian believes that God is a unity, He is One, and this is the creed which is rooted in the Old Testament, 'Hear O Israel, the Lord your God is one God'. This belief continues in the life of the church today. The Nicene Creed, which is recited in most liturgical churches every Sunday, begins with the words, 'We believe in One God'. Jesus himself taught the Lord's Prayer which is clearly monotheist, addressing God as 'Our Father'.

Trinitarianism, therefore, is not polytheism (more than one god), but rather an understanding of how the one God revealed himself throughout history. The doctrine of the unity of God allows for the existence of a complex divinity, which, while manifesting many parts, still constitutes one being.

Arab Christians living in the Arabian Peninsula have for many years sought ways to explain this to their Muslim counterparts. My personal favourite comes from an Arabic children's lesson from the ninth century. It teaches young people that God is like the sun. The sun consists of the ball, which radiates light and heat, and although these qualities are clearly different, they all radiate from and are of the same substance. Other examples include the egg, which consists of shell, white and yolk, or one person who carries the distinct roles of father, son, and office employee.

Illustrations in themselves mean nothing unless there are grounds to believe that Trinity is part of divine revelation. Do the scriptures back up such a concept? There must be some religious context, which would allow for a widespread acceptance of Trinity in the early church. Trinitarian thought did not emerge in a cultural or religious vacuum.

Christians believe that both the Old Testament and the New Testament, while not containing the actual word 'trinity' reveal the activity of a God who is a complex, unified oneness. They find this evidence running throughout scripture from the use of the plural pronoun found in Genesis where God speaks of himself as 'we' and 'us',[6] which is incidentally also found in the Qur'an when Allah frequently referred to his revelation in terms of the *pluralis majesticus* (the royal we). The Hebrew name of God in Genesis is *Elohim*, which is a plural form.

When God created mankind, he made mankind in his own image, which was both male and female.[7]

Robert Morey highlights that there are nine words in Hebrew, which denote oneness or unity, and only one of them is ever used to describe a solitary, indivisible mono-unit. This word is never used to describe God in the Old Testament. Instead, other Hebrew words are used which imply the concept of a unity of parts. Thus the creed of the Jewish faith can properly be translated as, 'Hear, O Israel: the Lord our God is *a unity*' (Deuteronomy 6:4).

Throughout the Old Testament, we read of the prophets having visions of God which always imply a complex unity. For example, when Abraham sees the 'the LORD' (a Jewish euphemism for seeing God) he sees three men. The following narrative makes no distinction between the three men and the Lord:

> The Lord appeared to Abraham near the great trees of Mamre while he was sitting at the entrance to his tent. Abraham looked up and saw three men standing nearby. Then the LORD said 'I will surely return to you next year'...

> then the three men got up to leave and Abraham walked
> alongside them when the LORD said... 'I will go down
> (to Sodom) and see what they have done. The men
> turned and went toward Sodom.'

> — Genesis 18: 1, 2, 10, 16, 20, 22

The great prophet Isaiah records his vision of God in the following words:

> In the year King Uzziah died, I saw the LORD seated on
> a throne, high and exalted and the train of his robe filled
> the temple. Above him were seraphs, each with six wings...
> and they were calling to each other 'Holy, Holy, Holy is
> the LORD almighty.' Then I heard the voice of the LORD
> saying 'Whom shall I send? And who will go for us?'

> — Isaiah 6: 1, 3, 8

We note that God is seen in anthropomorphic terms (a human figure sitting on a throne).[8] We see that the angels had a threefold doxology ('Holy, Holy, Holy...') and that the Lord asks, 'Who will go for us?'

Jeremiah, another major prophet in the Old Testament, describes how the word of the Lord would come to him in the form of a conversation with the LORD who appeared in human form.[9] See for example the following:

> Then the Lord reached out his hand and touched
> my mouth.
> — Jeremiah 1:9

Daniel (he of the lion's den fame) described his vision of God:

And there before me was one like a son of man,
coming with the clouds of heaven. He approached the
Ancient of Days and was led into his presence. He was
given authority, glory and sovereign power; all peoples,
nations and men of every language worshipped him.
His dominion is an everlasting dominion that will
not pass away, and his kingdom is one that will never
be destroyed.

— Daniel 7:13–14

Here in the Old Testament, we see a picture of God that is complex. At the heart of each vision is a human like figure who is 'like a son of man'[10] who is given divine status (to rule over a kingdom that is eternal).

There are numerous examples to be found in many of the Old Testament books, but all this goes to demonstrate that the idea of God manifesting in plural forms is built into the monotheism of the Bible.[11] This is far from a description of what God is really like, and we must be careful to recognize the limitations of human language in describing the mystery of God.

Karl Rahner, in his classic study, *The Trinity*, argues that the Bible reveals the economy (the works) of a God who is a complex unity and cautions against the futility of describing the ontology of God (ontology meaning to describe 'the real substance of'). In other words, the Christian believes in trinity because the Bible consistently reveals the workings of God who is Father, Son, and Holy Spirit.

So despite the monotheism of the Jewish faith, there is a theology which reveals God as a complex unity who has a history of intervening in history through manifesting himself in human form. It is this theology in which Jesus roots his claims. He especially refers to Isaiah.

Isaiah is famous for the 'suffering servant'[12] prophecies which Christians see as mirroring the life of Jesus. Jesus himself alluded to the words of Isaiah as describing his mission and identity. At the beginning of his ministry, he read the following scripture:

> The spirit of the LORD is on me, because he has anointed me to proclaim good news to the poor. He has sent me to proclaim freedom to the prisoners and recovery of sight for the blind, to set the oppressed free, to proclaim the year of the Lord's favour. Then he rolled up the scroll, gave it back to the attendant and sat down. The eyes of everyone in the synagogue were fastened on him. He began by saying to them, 'Today, this scripture is fulfilled in your hearing.'[13]
>
> – Luke 4:18–21

The Isaiah passages sum up the hopes and expectations of the Jewish people for God to send a Messiah who would usher in and rule the Kingdom of God. The nature of the Messiah, in terms of his task and character, imply that this is none other than God himself. This was clearly understood by the people who were listening to Jesus and they were deeply offended by his words. Their reaction was to try and punish Jesus for blasphemy.[14] During the trial of Jesus, which resulted in his death, the priests found him guilty of blasphemy, that is, claiming to be God:

> Again the high priest asked him, 'Are you the Messiah, the Son of the Blessed One?'
>
> 'I am,' said Jesus. 'And you will see the Son of Man sitting at the right hand of the Mighty One and coming on the clouds of heaven.'

The high priest tore his clothes. 'Why do we need
any more witnesses?' he asked. 'You have heard
the blasphemy.'

— Mark 14:61–64

Jesus was found guilty of claiming to be divine. A claim
the Gospel writers consistently show was at the heart of
His teachings and miracles. To extricate all the words
and actions from the New Testament books, which affirm
Jesus' divine status, would leave a document ragged
beyond description. The suggestion that 'proof' texts for
the doctrine of the Trinity (including Christ's divinity) were
inserted into scriptures would have required a rewrite. This
is simply not substantiated by textual evidence.

This is an extremely brief overview of some scriptural
evidences convincing Christians to believe that the trinity
is a valid description of the work and identity of God. The
same scripture in turn leads Christians to worship Jesus as
the divine Messiah, the embodiment of the one LORD who
reveals himself as a complex unity.

It is worth noting the philosophical debate surrounding
the nature of Christ as there has been a comparable discussion relating to the nature of the Qur'an. In essence, the
question focuses on the divine attributes of God and asks
whether or not a finite being can share in those attributes.

The Muta'zilite scholars of Baghdad in the tenth century argued that, as only God can be eternal, no created
object can. In applying this to the Qur'an, the debate surrounded the question of whether the Qur'an is the 'eternal'
uncreated word of God or a 'created' entity separate from
God. The Muta'zlites concluded that, as only God is eternal and there is only one of Him, then to attribute eternal
and uncreated status to anything or anyone else would be
to commit the sin of *shirk*, the grave crime of attributing
divine status to something besides God. Therefore the

Qur'an cannot be eternal. The implications of this con-clusion were not palatable for the more orthodox Islamic scholars who did not want to diminish the role and status of the Qur'an as a divine revelation. The end result was a brutal suppression of the Muta'zilite school of thought. However, Muta'zilite thought highlighted the whole area of divine attributes and explored the limitations of a rigid understanding of the oneness of God.[15]

So for example, if the 'word' of God is eternal, it implies something extra to God which shares an attribute which only God is allowed to have. We then face the challenge that God must be a composition of several divine attributes including mercy, compassion, and justice.

For the Christian, divine attributes, such as love, must imply a complex divine unity. The very nature of love requires an 'other' who must share in the divine nature of eternity. For love to exist, there must be a 'lover' and the object (beloved) of the lover. For love to be eternal, the lover and the beloved must also be eternal as indeed the medium, that is; the means by which the love is expressed between the lover and the beloved. The same applies to the attributes of compassion, mercy, and justice. For these qualities to be eternal there must be eternal 'others' who are the objects of the aforementioned mercy, compassion, and justice. If God is a perfect, solitary, indivisible unit, then these attri-butes cannot exist eternally and in effect become meaning-less categories. Perfection, by its very definition cannot be added to or taken away from – it is a static concept involving absolutely no change. The attributes of God are dynamic, always engaging with the changing world. Justice is imple-mented in response to negative behaviour. Mercy is unde-served kindness shown to a transgressor. The doctrine of Trinity, or an understanding of God who is a unity of these attributes, thus allows love and mercy and grace and His word to be eternal expressions of the divine character.

This allows the Biblical teaching of Jesus to be consistent with an understanding of God who has several eternal components. The Johannine declaration encapsulates this:

> In the beginning was the Word, and the Word was with God, and the Word was God. He was with God in the beginning. Through him all things were made; without him nothing was made that has been made. In him was life, and that life was the light of all mankind.

> The Word became flesh and made his dwelling among us.

> – John 1: 1–4, 14

Jesus was manifest as the eternal Word of God in human form and therein lies one of the main differences between Islam and Christianity. The eternal Word of God in Islam was revealed as a book, but for the Christian, it was a person. The Muta'zilite scholarship would have been scandalized by either of the last two propositions. Only God is eternal, not His Word or any of His other attributes. Their brutal repression by Orthodox Islam, oddly enough, opened the way for the eternal attributes of God to be recognized in a way which resonates deeply with Christian theology. At the most fundamental level, a God who is a being of many parts is a God who can communicate and relate to his creation. Revelation itself would be impossible for a God who is a singularity, for in order for God to reveal Himself, it is necessary that He requires eternal attributes which are dynamic and relative.

---

1   Sura 5:116
2   The word 'incarnation' implies that God dwelled in the flesh (carnal) and lived among human society.
3   Reported by Ayoub, M., 1984, p. 64.
4   Ibid. p. 64.

5 Sura 1: 1–7. As interpreted by N. J. Dawood: *The Koran* (London: Penguin Classics, 1999).

6 Genesis 1:26

7 Genesis 1:27

8 The Quran also contains anthropomorphic references to God. Various schools of theology within Islam deal with the anthropomorphic references to God in different ways. Most Sunni theological traditions believe that they are in some sense literal; that, for example, on the day of Judgement the believers will actually be able to see God's face and that God will have a corporeal body. The Muta'zilites (modern day Ibadis), on the other hand, believe that the anthropomorphic references are strictly metaphorical and that God cannot exist in bodily form, for to do so would be shirk.

9 The use of anthropomorphisms to describe God is a controversial issue in both Christianity and Islam. John Calvin vehemently rejected any suggestion that God had any human likeness as did several Islamic schools, most notably the Ibadi School of Islam found in Oman. See Valerie Hoffman, *The Essentials of Ibadi Islam* (USA: Syracuse University Press, 2011), pp. 31–33 for a discussion on anthropomorphisms.

10 This was the most common way in which Jesus described himself. Islamic scholars see this term as Jesus saying I am a human being, whereas to his Jewish audience, the term 'Son of Man' resonated with prophetic meaning and implications of divinity.

11 The use of the 'royal we' (the *pluralis majesticus*) is a common feature in semitic languages when referring to God. Both the Bible and the Holy Quran use plural forms when God speaks. Early Christian theologians understood the plural pronoun to refer to the Trinity. It remains a debate as to whether the plural form is making a statement about the essence of God or is simply a grammatical structure.

12 Isaiah 42, 43, 49

13 Jesus is reading the words of Isaiah 61:1–2 which speaks of a day when the Lord will restore salvation and righteousness to His people.

14 Luke 4:28–29

15 It is worth noting that Ibadis are the modern day Muta'zilite and may be the only existing school of theology that still believes in the created nature of the Quran.

APPENDIX D
THE BIBLE ON ARABS AND ARABIA

W HEN WE LOOK AT Arabia, we see that there is a long history in the region which is intricately woven into the story of the Church today. In fact, the very first book of the Bible records events which took place in what is now believed to be the Northern part of the Gulf, including Bahrain and Kuwait. With the rise and fall of ancient empires, the culture and languages would have been merged, adapted, and passed on to this very day. As Edward Said outlined in his seminal work on culture:

> Partly because of empire, all cultures are involved in one another, none is single and pure, all are hybrid, heterogeneous, extraordinarily differentiated, and unmonolithic.[1]

ABRAHAM: FRIEND OF GOD

A pivotal character in the faith history of Judaism, Christianity, and Islam is Abraham. All three faiths point to him as an inspirational man of faith. Centuries later, we find that the story of Abraham is one of the unifying motifs which draws Jews, Christians, and Muslims together in interfaith dialogue. At the heart of the life of Abraham is one of the most stunning promises made by God to a human being:

> I will make your name great,
> and you will be a blessing.
> I will bless those who bless you,
> and whoever curses you I will curse;
> and all peoples on earth
> will be blessed through you.
>
> – Genesis 12:2–3

The birthplace of Abraham was Ur, the principal city in that region. The kings of Ur ruled over and traded within an area that united the region from Kuwait up the valley of Tigris and Euphrates and across Syria to the Mediterranean. There are ancient Jewish traditions that suggest that Abraham travelled East and then South down through Arabia. Could the Gulf have been a region in which Abraham trod? The significance of Abraham increases because the Genesis story reveals that the Arabs of northern Arabia are descendants of Abraham through Ishmael. Therefore, we can see that some of the Arabs who live in Arabia today can trace their physical and spiritual roots back to Abraham himself. The promise of Abraham is shared with Ishmael.

The Biblical account of Abraham narrates the complicated origins of the Arab peoples. Abraham was married to Sarah who was not able to conceive, so she gave her servant Hagar to Abraham as a concubine. Hagar gave birth to Abraham's first born son, Ishmael.

Shortly after this, Hagar fled from Sarah and in the desert she encountered the Angel of the Lord who persuaded her to return back to Abraham, but not before promising her that her descendants would be too numerous to count.

God then instructs Abraham to circumcise every male in his family as sign of the covenant. The first male to be circumcised was Ishmael. The practice of circumcision continues to this day among the descendants of Abraham.

Meanwhile, Sarah, as a result of a promise from God, then gave birth to Isaac. Shortly after this, Hagar and Ishmael were banished to the desert. In the heat of the barren desert and with no water, Hagar found herself in a desperate situation. Fearing she was going to die, she abandoned Ishmael and cried out to God. The Angel of the Lord heard her cries, met with her, and promised her that Ishmael would be the source of a great nation. The Angel then opened her eyes to see a well of water and in this way she and the child survived. Ishmael grew up to become an archer and he lived in the desert of Paran. Hagar found him a wife from Egypt.

Isaac and Ishmael were later reconciled through the death of their father Abraham.

THE DESCENDANTS OF ABRAHAM

The descendants of Ishmael are recorded twice in Scripture (Genesis 25 and I Chronicles 1) along with the descendants of Isaac. This indicates their involvement with the covenant blessing of God. It is believed that one of the sons of Ishmael, Mishima, is the ancestor of the Saudi Arabian tribe the Beni Misma. Another son of Ishmael, Mibsam, is probably the founder of the Nejdi tribe of Bessam Kedar. Yet another son of Ishmael (according to the narrative of Scripture) is the generic name in the Old Testament for the bedouin.

The Kedar emerge several times in the Old Testament and we know that they relate to the descendants of Ishmael who were the Arabs of the desert and the ancestors of the Kuwaiti people today. Below is a list of Biblical references to the people of Kedar. To the people of Islam, the Kedar is also significant as they are said to be the ancestors of the Prophet Muhammad.

More significantly for the Gulf region is that scholars can link some of the local tribes back to Ishmael through his first son, Nebaioth. Nebaioth gave birth to Adnan from whom the Adnani tribes descend. Abu Hakima succinctly summarizes the link:

> All authorities writing agree that the 'Utub belong to 'Anaza, an Adnani tribe, inhabiting Najd and Northern Arabia. The Al-Sabah family (in Kuwait) for example claim to be a division of 'Anaza.

The Abrahamic link is therefore more than a spiritual one. Through the pages of the Old Testament we see a reminder of the role Arabs play in Biblical history. It is worth remembering that some of the Biblical stories are about the ancestors of the Gulf Arabs today.

Throughout the Old Testament there are constant references to the Arab Nation, the descendents of Ishmael. They are linked to the Israelite people through trade, warfare, poetry, and prophecy as the following selection of texts reveal.

ARABS AND TRADE

> Not including the revenues from merchants and traders and from all the Arabian kings and the governors of the land.
>
> – Kings 10:15

Some Philistines brought Jehoshaphat gifts and silver
as tribute, and the Arabs brought him flocks: seven
thousand seven hundred rams and seven thousand
seven hundred goats.

— Chronicles 17:11

Arabia and all the princes of Kedar were your customers;
they did business with you in lambs, rams and goats.

— Ezekiel 27:21

Not including the revenues brought in by merchants and
traders. Also all the kings of Arabia and the governors of
the territories brought gold and silver to Solomon.

— Chronicles 9:14

ARABS IN TENSION AND WARFARE

The LORD aroused against Jehoram the hostility of the
Philistines and of the Arabs who lived near the Cushites.

— Chronicles 21:16

Since the raiders, who came with the Arabs into the
camp, had killed all the older sons. So Ahaziah son
of Jehoram king of Judah began to reign.

— Chronicles 22:1

God helped him against the Philistines and against the
Arabs who lived in Gur Baal and against the Meunites.

— Chronicles 26:7

ARABS AND BIBLICAL ALLEGORIES

Look up to the barren heights and see. Is there any place where you have not been ravished? By the roadside you sat waiting for lovers, sat like an Arab in the desert.

— Jeremiah 3:2

Dark am I, yet lovely, daughters of Jerusalem, dark like the tents of Kedar, like the tent curtains of Solomon.

— Song of Solomon 1:5

ARABS AND PROPHECIES

The Arabs would inhabit the Arabian peninsula, the wilderness of Paran, or in Arabic, Faran.

— Genesis 21:21

All Kedar's flocks will be gathered to you, the rams of Nebaioth will serve you; they will be accepted as offerings on my altar, and I will adorn my glorious temple.

— Isaiah 60:7

As we see from the above selection, the Arabs were very much interwoven into the Biblical story of God's work in the Middle East and the Gulf.

GEOGRAPHICAL SETTINGS OF BIBLE STORIES

The climate in Arabia has not always been harsh and the terrain has not always been desert. Millions of years ago, most of the Gulf was in fact dry land and was covered by great forests (which is now the source of the oil fields). The sea was around 300 metres below the present levels since much of the water was frozen in the great ice caps. As the climate warmed, the ice caps melted and the sea levels began to rise, thus forming the shape of the Gulf today.

Eden means a plain or flat place[2]. In the book of Genesis chapter two, it states:

> Now the Lord God had planted a garden in the east,
> in Eden... A river watering the garden flowed from
> Eden; from there it was separated into four headwaters.
> The name of the first is the Pishon; it winds through the
> entire land of Havilah where there is gold. (The gold of
> that land is good; aromatic resin and onyx are also there.)
> The name of the second river is the Gihon; it winds
> through the entire land of Cush. The name of the third
> river is the Tigris; it runs along the east side of Ashur.
> And the fourth river is the Euphrates.
>
> – Genesis 2:8,10–14

The latter two rivers are located in the north of the Gulf flowing through modern day Iraq. So the latter rivers are known to us, but where are the other two rivers mentioned in Genesis?

Scholars are divided but generally it is suggested that there are two possible locations. Michael Sanders suggests that the Garden of Eden is located at the northern end of the Euphrates and this places it in the far eastern region of modern Turkey. This theory is not widely shared. The most compelling evidence for the location of the Garden of Eden is provided by Juris Zarins who revives a popular view held in the eighteenth century but this time uses satellite photography to support his case.

Zarins goes back to geography and geology to pinpoint the area of Eden where he believes the river collision came to a head. The evidence is beguiling. First, Genesis was written from a Hebrew point of view. It says the garden was 'eastward', that is to say, east of Israel. It is quite specific about the rivers. The Tigris and the Euphrates are easy because they still flow. At the time Genesis was written, the Euphrates must have been the major one because it stands identified by name only and without an explanation about what it 'winds through'. The Pishon can be identified from the Biblical reference to the land of Havilah, which is easily located in the Biblical Table of Nations (Genesis 10:7, 25:18) as relating to localities and people within a Mesopotamian–Arabian framework. Geological evidence on the ground and LANDSAT images from space support the Biblical evidence of Havilah. These images clearly show a 'fossil river', that once flowed through northern Arabia and through the now dry beds which modern Saudis and Kuwaitis know as the Wadi Riniah and the Wadi Batin. Furthermore, as the Bible says, this region was rich in bdellium, an aromatic gum resin that can still be found in north Arabia, and gold, which was still mined in the general area in the 1950s.

It is the Gihon, which 'winds through the entire land of Cush', that has been the problem. In Hebrew, the geographical reference was to 'Gush' or 'Kush'. The translators of the King James Bible in the seventeenth century rendered Gush or Kush as 'Ethiopia', which is further to the south and in Africa – thus upsetting the geographical applecart and flummoxing researchers for centuries. Zarins now believes the Gihon is the Karun River, which rises in Iran and flows southwesterly toward the present Gulf. The Karun also shows in LANDSAT images and was a perennial river which, until it was dammed, contributed, along with the Tigris and Euphrates, most of the sediment forming the delta at the head of the Persian Gulf.

Thus the Garden of Eden, on geographical evidence, may have been somewhere at the head of the Gulf at a time when all four rivers joined and flowed through an area that was then above the level of the Gulf. The wording in Genesis that Eden's river 'separated into four headwaters' was dealt with by Biblical scholar Ephraim Speiser some years ago. The passage, he said, refers to the four rivers upstream of their confluence into the one river watering the Garden. This is a strange perspective, but understandable if one reflects that the description is of a folk memory, written millennia after the events encapsulated, by men who had never been within leagues of the territory.

This is not a new theory, and further evidence is suggested by studies of the Dilmun Empire (3200–1600 BC) believed to have been based in Bahrain. This ancient civilization points to some of the early city dwellers known in history. Older cities have been identified in the region in Ur and in 'Ubaid, which reach back to the fifth millennium BC). There appear to be ancient ruins under the waters of the Gulf, suggesting that there was a time when humans could traverse around the Gulf much more on land than is possible now. Geological evidence shows that the Gulf extended much further North in the 'Ubaid period. Extensive studies show the gradual stages of the infilling of the Gulf taking place from 10,000 BC, following on from the end of the last Ice Age. Some archaeologists speculate this is the origins of the Gilgamesh mythology which is mirrored in the later Biblical story of Noah and the flood. This is yet another link between the Gulf and the early parts of the Old Testament.

Archaeologists are agreed that some of the earliest city-dwelling civilizations in the Gulf came from the Sumerian people who travelled down to the Gulf from Mesopotamia and possibly settled in the region, or that the Sumerians were trading with established local communities. The Dilmun Empire revealed that they were trading along the Gulf coast and evidence of their presence has been found in Failaka, Kuwait, extensive parts of the UAE and in Bahrain. Adam and Eve's progeny, Cain, is recorded in Genesis as building a city, and presumably this would have been somewhere near the vicinity of the Garden of Eden. Given that some of the earliest settlements are found in the Gulf, this might suggest a tenuous link between the Dilmun Empire and the account of Genesis. This is a tenuous link because there were other empires besides Dilmun. For example there is evidence of trade between the Harappa empire and the Gulf.

However speculative many of the reports are with regards to the Garden of Eden location, there is without doubt a wide consensus from scholars that it may have been located somewhere in the Northern Gulf. It is quite possible that wanderings of the Biblical Cain would have taken him through the area that we now know as Kuwait.

Some of the better known stories of the Old Testament highlighted that many of these took place in Arabian regions and empires which would have included the area where Kuwait is today. One of these stories includes Jonah, the reluctant prophet who took on the unenviable task of confronting an empire. Nineveh was the last principal city of the Assyrian Empire and it was in this city that Jonah proclaimed his message of 'repent or perish'. To Jonah's great disappointment, the Ninevites responded to his message and imminent judgment was deferred. The Kings of Ninevah ruled a vast area that included the land of Kuwait. The Assyrian Empire dominated the region from 750 BC through to 600 BC.

While the Assyrian kings were looting the lands to the east and oppressing the people of Israel, a hardy desert people called the 'Kaldi' had, for centuries, been creeping around the Arabian Gulf and possibly settling along the shores.

In the northern mountains, a tribe called the Medes had been growing in power. They formed an alliance with the Kaldi (known to us as Chaldeans) and they finally took Babylon from Assyria. From there they moved to take over Ninevah and the great Assyrian Empire quickly unravelled. The rise of the Babylonian empire replaced the Assyrian rule and in time took over the vast area. Neo-Babylonia (626–539 BC) was ruled by a succession of Chaldean kings of which the best known was Nebuchadnezzar the Second with whom the Biblical character Daniel was associated.

Following the disastrous rule of Belshazzar, Darius the Mede ushered in the Medo Persian empire (539–330 BC). He was followed by the great ruler Cyrus, the King of Persia. In 539 BC Cyrus led his conquering hosts against Babylonia. It turned out to be surprisingly easy. The gates of Babylon were opened wide to the Persians and the captive Hebrews were filled with joy.

It was during the reign of Cyrus that Ezra the priest led a return of Jews back to Jerusalem. The story of Esther and Mordecai was set in the rule of the Persian King, Xerxes, who ruled from 485–465 BC. During this time, armies and traders would cross the Northern Gulf between Persia and Babylonia.

The Persian empire finally fell to the Greek empire led by Alexander the Great in 330 BC. Ruins of a Greek colony on Failaka island show evidence of the Alexandrian campaign eastwards. Thereafter, the Greek empire fractured and was gradually subsumed by the Roman Empire which, however, did not come as far east as the Gulf and so the Persians restated their control over this region. It is during this time that a child was born in Bethlehem. The Roman Empire had control of the Levant and used Idumean kings as puppets in order to maintain control. The notorious Herodian dynasty were among the local kings exploited by the Roman Empire and it was on their watch that the story of Jesus played out. His preaching and teaching, life, death, and resurrection triggered a movement that came to be known as Christianity.

ARABS IN THE NEW TESTAMENT

The New Testament has far fewer references to Arabs than the Old Testament, yet there are two significant mentions of Arabs. Firstly, we read that Arabs were present at the Day of Pentecost (Acts 2:11) and Arabic was one of the tongues spoken.

We can only speculate about what the Arabs made of the Pentecost events and whether they were among the three thousand who chose baptism that day. Did the message of the Christian faith enter Arabia from that time? We know from the book of Acts that an Ethiopian travelling down through the Sinai desert road was responsible for taking the Gospel to Ethiopia (now home to one of the oldest churches in the world). What the book of Acts does imply is that there were Jewish Arabic speaking communities in Arabia and that these Arab Jews were in Jerusalem to celebrate the first fruits of harvest and to remember the giving of the Mosaic law. Perhaps more significant, with regards to Kuwait, was that there is mention of 'Parthians, Medes and Elamites (Acts 2:9); residents of Mesopotamia' describing people from Southern Iraq and Southern Iran.

Secondly, there is a reference to Arabia linked with St Paul. Galatians gives a tantalizingly brief mention of St Paul's time away in Arabia after his Damascus road conversion (Galatians 1:17). Newby speculates that Paul must have retreated to an Essene-type community where, after being immersed in the Old Testament scriptures, he burst back onto the main arena with a convincing apologia, in which Jesus is linked with the eschatological Messianic figure of the Jewish scriptures.

Through the ministry of Paul, the Christian message expanded beyond the Jewish communities and was carried to all corners of the known world. What is little known is that while Saint Paul was expanding the Church in the west, there were already churches forming to the east as a result of the apostles Thomas, Thaddeus, and Bartholemew, and that this Church of the East expanded into more countries and involved more people than the Church of the West. In fact, the Church of the East (also known as the Nestorian Church) eclipsed the Western church in terms of size and scale of mission. Baumer, a well-established scholar of the Eastern Church, estimates that during the tenth to the fourteenth centuries there were approximately seven to eight million Nestorians scattered across 200 Dioceses:

> Until the start of the fourteenth century, the Church of
> the East was the most successful missionary Church in
> the world, and it began to be surpassed only in the
> sixteenth century through the conversions, often forced,
> brought about by the catholic colonial powers.[3]

Several authors[4] have traced the history of the Christian Church in the Middle East and have commented on the ancient traditions, which have been preserved through the liturgies, Bible commentaries, and a worldview still discernible today.

We can conclude then that the Bible and Arabia are closely connected. The teachings of Jesus were carried initially in Aramaic and Greek, and then very early on in the history of the Church the Gospel was communicated in the medium of Syriac and Arabic. Due to the similarities of the languages and shared geographical climates, the cultural frame of reference, which undergirds Jesus' teachings resonates with shared meanings.

1   Edward Said, *Culture and Imperialism* (New York: Vintage, 1994), p. xxv.
2   For a more complete discussion of the location of the garden of Eden see D. J. Hamblin, 'Has the Garden of Eden been located at last?' *Smithsonian Magazine*, Vol. 18, No. 2, 1987.
3   Baumer, C., *The Church of the East: An Illustrated History of Assyrian Christianity* (I.B. Taurus: London, 2006). p. 4.
4   See William Dalrymple, Robert Brenton Betts, Kenneth Cragg, Betty Jane Bailey & J. Martin Bailey, Christoph Baumer and J. Spencer Trimingham.

BIBLIOGRAPHY

Abdel Haleem, M. A. S., *The Qur'an: A New Translation* (Oxford: Oxford University Press, 2004)

Al Habtoor, K. A., *Khalaf Ahmad Al Habtoor: The Autobiography* (Dubai: Motivate Publishing, 2012)

Al Omari, J., *The Arab Way* (Oxford: How to Books, 2003)

Al Mansoori, K.A., *The Distinctive Arab Heritage: A Study of Society, Culture and Sport in the UAE* (Abu Dhabi: Emirates Heritage Club, 2004)

Alsharekh, A, & Springborg, R., *Popular Culture and Political Identity in the Arab Gulf States* (London, SOAS, 2008)

Allen, M., *Arabs* (London: Continuum, 2006)

Allison, M.B., *Doctor Mary in Arabia* (Austin: University of Texas Press, 1994)

Arberry, A. J., *The Koran Interpreted* (Oxford: Oxford University Press, 1964)

Asher, M., *The Last of the Bedu: In Search of the Myth* (London: Penguin Books, 1996)

Aslan, R., *No god but God: The Origins, Evolution, and Future of Islam* (New York: Random House, 2011)

Aslan, R., *Zealot: The Life and Times of Jesus of Nazareth* (New York: Random House, 2013)

Ayoub, M., *The Qur'an and its Interpreters* Vol.I (New York: University of New York Press, 1984)

Bailey, B.J. & M.B., *Who are the Christians in the Middle East?* (Michigan: Eerdmans, 2003)

Bailey, K.E., *Jesus Through Middle Eastern Eyes: Cultural Studies in the Gospels*. (London: SPCK, 2008)

Bailey, K.E., *Poet & Peasant and Through Peasant Eyes*. (Michigan: Eerdmans, 1983)

Barclay, W., *The Gospel of Luke* (Edinburgh: The Saint Andrew Press, 1975)

Barclay, W., *The Gospel of John. Vol 1*. (Edinburgh, The Saint Andrew Press, 1975)

Barclay, W., *The Gospel of John. Vol 2*. (Edinburgh, The Saint Andrew Press, 1975)

Baumer, C., *The Church of the East. An Illustrated History of Assyrian Christianity*. (London: I.B. Taurus, 2006)

Bell, R., *The Qur'an Translated with a Critical Rearrangement of the Surahs* (Edinburgh: T & T Clark, 1937)

Bell, R., *Velvet Elvis: Repainting the Christian Faith* (Michigan: Zondervan, 2005)

Benesh, G. C., *Culture Shock. A Survival Guide to Customs and Etiquette. United Arab Emirates* (New York: Marchall Canvendish Corporation, 2009)

Betts, R. B., *Christians in the Arab East* (Atlanta: John Knox Press, 1978)

Brock, S. P., *Syriac Writers from Beth Qatraye*. (ARAM periodical 11/12, 2000)

Caton. C. S., *Yemen Chronicle: An Anthropology of War and Mediation* (New York: Hill & Wang, 2005)

Clements, R., *A Sting in the Tale* (Leicester: IVP, 1995)

Cooper, A., *Ishmael: My Brother*. (Bromley: MARC Europe, 1985)

Cragg, K., *The Arab Christian: A History in the Middle East*. (Kentucky: John Knox Press, 1991)

Dalrymple, W., *From the Holy Mountain: A Journey among the Christians of the Middle East*. (London: Holt Paperbacks, 1999)

Davidson, C. M., *Abu Dhabi: Oil and Beyond* (London: Hurst & Company, 2009)

Dawood, N. J. (trans). *The Koran* (London: Penguin Classics, 1999)

Deedat, A., *The Choice: Islam and Christianity, Vol. 1* (South Africa: Islamic Propagation Centre, 1993)

Dupont-Sommer, A., *The Essene Writings from Qumran* (USA: Peter Smith Publisher Inc., 1973)

Ford, D. F., *The Promise of Scriptural Reasoning*. (Oxford: Wiley-Blackwell, 2006)

Freeman, J. M., *Manners and Customs of the Bible* (New Jersey: Bridge Publishing, 1972)

Green, J. B. McKnight, S. & Marshall, H. (Eds), *Dictionary of Jesus and the Gospels. A Compendium of Contemporary Biblical Scholarship* (Leicester: IVP, 1992)

Griffith, S. H., *The Bible in Arabic: The Scriptures of the 'People of the Book' in the Language of Islam* (Princeton: Princeton University Press, 2013)

Guiness, M., *Woman: The Full Story* (Michigan: Zondervan, 2003)

Hamblin, D. J., 'Has the Garden of Eden been located at last?' *Smithsonian Magazine* Volume 18. No2. 1987

Hayes, A., *Footsteps of Thesiger* (Dubai: Motivate Publishing, 2012)

Hellyer, P & Ziolkowski, M., *Emirates Heritage: Volume One. Proceedings of the 1ˢᵗ Annual Symposium on Recent Palaeontological & Archaeological Discoveries in the Emirates* (Al Ain: Zayed Centre for Heritage and History, 2005)

Hicks, J., *The Myth of God Incarnate* (London: SCM Press, 1977)

Hitti, P., *History of the Arabs*. 10ᵗʰ Edition (London: Palgrave-MacMillan, 2002)

Hoffman, V. J., *The Essentials of Ibadi Islam* (USA: Syracuse University Press, 2011)

Holton, P., *Mother Without a Mask* (London: Kyle Cathie Limited, 1991)

Hourani, A., *A History of the Arab Peoples* (London: Faber & Faber, 1991)

Huntington, S. P. *The Clash of Civilizations and the Remaking of World Order* (New York: Simon & Schuster, 1996)

Insoll, T., *Land of Enki in the Islamic: Pearls, Palms and Religious Identity in Bahrain* (London: Routledge, 2005)

Johnson, B., *When Heaven Invades Earth* (Shippensburg: Destiny Image Publishers Inc., 2003)

Johnson, L. T., *The Real Jesus: The Misguided Quest for the Historical Jesus and the Truth of the Traditional Gospels* (San Francisco: Harper, 1997)

Kaiser Jr, W.C., *The Old Testament Documents. Are They Reliable and Relevant?* (India: OM Books, 2003)

Khalidi, T., *The Muslim Jesus: Sayings and Stories in Islamic Literature* (London: Harvard University Press, 2001)

Lawson, T., *The Crucifixion and the Qur'an: A Study in the History of Muslim Thought* (Oxford: Oneworld, 2009)

Lewis, C.S., 2009 *Mere Christianity* (San Francisco: Harper, Revised and Enlarged Edition, 2009)

Loosley, E., *A Historical Overview of the Arabian Gulf into the Late Pre-Islamic Period: The Evidence for Christianity in the Gulf.* (Abu Dhabi: Abu Dhabi Islands Archaeological Survey, 2002)

Mallouhi, C.A., *Waging Peace on Islam.* (London: Monarch Books, 2000)

McAuliffe, J. (eds)., *The Encyclopaedia of the Qur'an* (Leiden: E.J. Brill, 2005)

Mingana, A.. 'The Apology of Timothy the Patriarch before the Caliph Mahdi.' *Bulletin of the John Rylands Library.* Vol 12. No.1. 1928. pp. 137–298.

Nader, L., *Culture and Dignity: Dialogues between the Middle East and the West.* (Oxford: Wiley & Blackwell, 2013)

Newbiggin, L., *Foolishness to the Greeks: The Gospel and Western Culture* (Michigan: Eerdmans Publishing Company, 1986)

Newby, G.D., *A History of the Jews of Arabia* (Columbia: University of South Carolina, 1988)

Nydell, M.K., *Understanding Arabs: A Guide for Westerners.* (Maine: Intercultural Press, 2002)

O'Sullivan, E., *The New Gulf: How Modern Arabia is Changing the World for Good* (Dubai: Motivate Publishing, 2008)

Parrinder, G., *Jesus in the Qur'an.* (London: Faber, 1965)

Perrin, N., *Lost in Transmission? What We Can Know About the Words of Jesus.* (Dallas: Thomas Nelson, 2007)

Poplak, R., *The Sheikh's Batmobile: In Pursuit of American Pop Culture in the Muslim World* (Canada: Penguin, 2009)

Ragg, L & L., *The Gospel of Barnabas* (Oxford: The Clarendon Press, 1907)

Raheb, M., *Sailing through Troubled Waters: Christianity in the Middle East* (Bethlehem, Diyar Publisher, 2013)

Rahner, K., *The Trinity* (Tunbridge Wells: Burns & Oates, 1986)

Rajab, J.S., *Failaka Island: The Ikaros of the Arabian Gulf.* (Kuwait: Tareq Rajab Museum, 2008)

Rippin, A., *Muslims: Their Religious Beliefs and Practices. Volume 2: The Contemporary Period.* (London: Routledge, 1993).

Robinson, N., *Discovering the Qur'an. A Contemporary Approach to a Veiled Text.* (London: SCM, 1996)

Rodinson, M., *The Arabs* (University of Chicago Press, 1981)

Rousseau, J.J. & Arav, R., *Jesus and His World: An Archaeological and Cultural Dictionary* (London: SCM Press, 1995)

Ryken, L. Wilhoit, J.C. & Longman III, T. (General Eds), *Dictionary of Biblical Imagery* (Leicester: IVP, 1988)

Sahih Al Bukhari (New Delhi: Islamic Book Service, 2004)

Said, E., *Orientalism* (New York: Vintage Books, 1979)

Said, E., *Culture and Imperialism* (New York: Vintage, 1994)

Sale, G., *The Koran: Translated into English from the Original Arabic* (London and New York: Frederick Warne & Co Ltd, 1734)

Sasson, J., *Princess: A True Story of Life behind the Veil in Saudi Arabia* (New York: Bantam Publishers, 2001)

Sheler, J. L., *Is the Bible True? How Modern Debates and Discoveries Affirm the Essence of the Scriptures* (London: Harper Collins Publishers, 1999)

Steinbeck, J., *The Pearl* (London: Puffin Books, 1947)

Sweetman, J. W., *Islam and Christian Theology. Vol. 1* (London: Lutterworth Press, 1945)

Swidler, L., *Women in Judaism* (New York: Scarecrow Press, 1976)

Thesiger, W., *Arabian Sands* (London: Longmans, 1959)

Thomson, A., *Jesus Prophet of Islam* (London: TaHa Publishers, 1977)

Thompson, A., *Christianity in the UAE: Culture and Heritage.* (Dubai: Motivate Publishing, 2011)

Torstrick, R. L. & Faier, E., *Culture and Customs of the Arab Gulf States* (London: Greenwood Press, 2009)

Trimingham, J. S., *Christianity among the Arabs in Pre-Islamic Times* (Beirut: Longman Group, 1979)

Volf, M., *Allah: A Christian Response* (New York: HarperOne, 2012)

Waardeburg, J., *Muslim Perceptions of Other Religions: A Historical Survey* (Oxford: Oxford University Press, 1999)

Wenham, D. *The Parables of Jesus* (Illnois: IVP, 1989)

Wilcox, M., *The Message of Luke* (Leicester: IVP, 1979)

Wilson, A.N., *Jesus: A Life* (New York: W.W. Norton & Company, 1992)

Witherington, B., *The Jesus Quest* (USA: IVP, 1997)

Wright, T., *Luke for Everyone* (London: SPCK, 2001)

Yusuf, Abdullah Ali, *The Holy Qur'an: Text Translation and Commentary*. (Kuwait: That Es Salasil, 1938)

Zogby, J., *Arab Voices: What they are Saying to Us and Why it Matters* (New York: Palgrave Macmillan, 2010)

INDEX